HOW TO
MURDER
YOUR WEALTHY
LOVERS
AND GET AWAY WITH IT

RED ⚡ LIGHTNING BOOKS

JANE SIMON AMMESON

HOW TO
MURDER
YOUR WEALTHY
LOVERS
AND GET AWAY WITH IT

MONEY & MAYHEM IN THE GILDED AGE

This book is a publication of

Red Lightning Books
1320 East 10th Street
Bloomington, Indiana 47405 USA
redlightningbooks.com

Manufactured in the United States of America

Cataloging information is available
from the Library of Congress.

ISBN 978-1-68435-024-7 (paperback)
ISBN 978-1-68435-055-1 (ebook)

1 2 3 4 5   23 22 21 20 19 18

CONTENTS

PROLOGUE   1

1   TRUE LOVE NEVER RUNS SMOOTH:
       THE DEATH OF A NEW GROOM   9

2   THERE IS A HOUSE
       IN NEW ORLEANS   29

3   DON'T CRY FOR ME, EMPORIA:
       GREAT BALLS OF FIRE!   45

4   PARDON MY DUST:
       NONSTOP TO NOWHERE   60

5   BLOOD MONEY SQUANDERED: THE NECESSITY
       OF CATCHING MR. KETCHAM   90

6   THE IMPORTANCE OF KEEPING
       MR. KETCHAM—AND HIS MONEY   102

7   THE COMPANY SHE KEEPS   113

8   MOVING ON UP: IN WHICH JOSEPHINE
           CAPTURES AND LOSES A PRINCE   131

9   OF PLUM JAM, CHAMPAGNE, WILLS,
           UNPAID BILLS, AND THE FINAL DEATH
           THAT WE KNOW OF   147

           BIBLIOGRAPHY   165

How To

MURDER

YOUR WEALTHY

LOVERS

AND GET AWAY WITH IT

PROLOGUE

WHEN MINNIE WALLACE WALKUP, JUST SIXTEEN YEARS old, went on trial for poisoning James R. Walkup, her much older, very wealthy husband, there were two things the public and reporters who covered the sensational 1885 trial in Emporia, Kansas, could agree on. The first was that Minnie was exceptionally beautiful—a luscious, ripe southern belle with hints of Creole heritage. The second was that she was always, from the moment of her husband's death, cool, collected, and composed.

How cool was she? Think glacier-like before global warming. But don't take our word for it. Here's how a reporter described the Walkup home on the day Walkup died after the autopsy was performed in couple's bedroom—yes, that's where they did them back then.

The Beauty's Heartlessness
Emporia Daily News, Tuesday, November 10, 1885

The doctors cut him to pieces, removing his liver, heart, stomach, in fact removing nearly everything else. The bed was in a frightful condition, the remains were scattered about the room in vessels, and the air was horrible, and yet within an hour after the body had been taken downstairs, the widow went to the room, still uncleaned, locked herself in and proceeded to undress herself as calmly as if there was no ghastly evidence of death within a hundred miles of her.

Now that's ice.

In late 1884, wealthy James Walkup, twice a widower, traveled from Emporia, Kansas, to New Orleans, ostensibly to attend the Cotton Exposition being held there that year but more likely to taste the delights of the Crescent City. He was fifty-two when he checked in to Elizabeth Wallace's boardinghouse at 222 Canal Street in the French Quarter. Mrs. Wallace's sensuously stunning daughter Minnie was only fifteen, but Walkup was thunderstruck and by the next morning had announced his intentions to marry her.

The courtship lasted longer than the marriage and required the bride-to-be and her mother to visit Emporia to check out Walkup's properties and prospects. About eight months after they first met, Minnie and James were married. A month to the day of their nuptials, an autopsy showed his gruesome death was due to arsenic poisoning.

John Ketcham, a rich Chicago clubman and Minnie's second groom, was in his sixties when she was twenty-seven or so. This marriage lasted somewhat longer—he made it two months after they married. Some thought his death might have been due to poison, but it was attributed to cirrhosis of the liver.

During his illness, Minnie had kept him virtually a prisoner in her home while keeping an apartment down the street where she entertained gentlemen callers.

Minnie wasn't married to her third lover, DeLancey Louderback, when he died of strychnine poisoning, though she was heir to a quarter of his once considerable estate. It was said that she'd sent him the vial of the poison to use as a sleeping draught. It sure did cause a deep, permanent slumber.

Why did she marry men old enough to be her grandfather?

"Their knowledge of life fascinates me," she replied to inquiring newsmen. "A man must know how to woo a woman to win me—and young men have not the experience."

She was less concise when asked by authorities why she bought the arsenic that had caused Walkup's death. Minnie had many stories. She couldn't remember buying it. She bought it to lighten her complexion. She needed it to mix with urine to take a stain out of her dress. Or maybe, she speculated, he had bought it and poisoned himself. Memory failed Minnie about what had happened, and the members of the all-male jury, though they didn't really believe her but hesitant to condemn a woman, voted to set her free.

In John Ketcham's last months, the doctors had tried to keep him from drinking. Minnie had a different theory of medicine. He needed the liquor she smuggled into his sickroom, she said when confronted with her actions, to keep him alive. When his angry relatives, sure that this black widow had killed him, asked where the will and marriage license were, she couldn't really remember.

Oh, there was so much she couldn't recall.

"I don't remember," she testified over and over, remaining composed while avoiding the truth. No, she really didn't recall asking the maid to say she was going out to buy butter when she went to purchase poison instead. She forgot entire conversations with two pharmacists who inquired why she was buying arsenic.

Besides amnesia, her other weapon was alternative fiction.

Canned oysters, not the arsenic she was stockpiling, were what ended Walkup's life on that hot August day. She probably had also forgotten that after he ingested the oysters, she volunteered to go downtown to buy him a soda pop, stopping at yet another drugstore. There she bought more poison—spending twenty-five cents for four ounces of a highly toxic type, though pharmacist Ben Wheldon told her that most ladies using arsenic to lighten their complexion bought Fowler's Solution, which contained less than 1 percent of the poison. She certainly forgot to sign the book stating the purpose for her purchase before she walked out.

But it didn't seem to really matter what lovely Minnie Wallace Walkup—she of the dark Madonna eyes, who was celebrated for her loveliness since she was very young—forgot. The all-male jury seemed enthralled, as did others in the courtroom, including the judge and John Jay, another older man who had promised his fortune to free her. Even when the evidence piled up against her and the courtroom crowd seemed to turn against her, Minnie was always able to win her audience back.

Sure, there was the incident with William Born, a neighbor who attended the wedding party when the new Mr. and Mrs. J. R. Walkup returned home. He developed symptoms of arsenic poisoning after accepting a beer from Walkup that Minnie had prepared for her husband. Born survived and later stated he believed he was the accidental victim of a dose meant for the new groom.

And yes, Minnie spent more time on sewing her mourning dress than in actually mourning the loss of her spouse.

When Dr. Jacobs, who had just come from the deathbed of her husband, asked to see all the powders she had collected from her many drugstore visits, she immediately agreed to fetch the box that she kept in her room.

But—oh, no!—as she was carrying the box in her finely shaped hands, it slipped from her grasp, the fine powders drifting all over the dress she was wearing and down the stairs she had been descending. While she tried scraping the spilled medicines back into the box (an impossible job), Dr. Jacobs, who suspected poison, took some of the particles for testing. Would you be surprised to learn that it was arsenic? No? We didn't think so.

It didn't matter. All who attended the trial always reverted to the impossibility of such a lovely widow committing such a heinous act. One of the male jurors told reporters he was haunted by the thought of sending the beautiful widow to the gallows.

As for the poisoning of DeLancy Louderback, a rich industrialist, which also took place in Chicago, authorities didn't even bother to charge her, despite testimony that she had supplied the vial containing the cyanamide that caused his death. Maybe they were tired of trying to get a jury to hold Minnie accountable.

The deaths laid at her feet didn't seem to slow her down.

She collected her inheritances, spending the money gleefully on lush living, expensive clothes (she liked to sparkle in jewels, form-fitting gowns, and peacock feathers when she went out on the town), and frequent trips to Europe. When money was tight, a new husband was found. When he died, she again lived lavishly. Between husbands, there were always men at her beck and call. A married former governor of Louisiana and US senator took her on a long trip out west after the jury in Emporia let her walk free. She was a niece, he sometimes told people, and Minnie said they were chaperoned by the senator's sister—though no one ever saw the woman at all. No one believed that story.

She was his daughter, said DeLancy Louderback when he traveled to Europe with Minnie and his desperately ill wife of thirty-three years, but no one believed that either.

DeLancy, before he ingested poison, spent $1 million just to furnish a house in Chicago he built for her (at a cost of another million), and when our Minnie decided she didn't want to live there—indeed, never set foot in the home after it was completed—he set her up in a tony place on Eighty-Eighth Street in New York City. He also gave her endless amounts of money, over $3 million in all.

If you're looking for stories with moral endings, of comeuppances resulting in poverty and despair or repentance, reform, and finding solace and peace in religion, the story of Minnie Wallace Walkup Ketcham Keating isn't for you.

If she was guilty of all she was accused of, then there wasn't any righteous payback. Minnie outlived all of her contemporaries.

The other beautiful but soiled doves she counted as her friends grew dissipated, their prettiness soon gone. Lacking financial sense and in the end their good looks, they were soon left with nothing.

Not Minnie. Though she disappeared from the relentless newspaper accounts of her first five decades, she lived to the grand old age of eighty-eight, dying on May 10, 1957, and was buried at Mount Hope Cemetery in San Diego her death certificate bearing the names she chose, somewhat oddly, at the end: "Estelle (aka Estella) Minnie Keating (aka Ketchum [*sic*])."

When I first started researching Minnie's story, I thought it was her exceptional beauty—which she held on to for so long in those days before Botox, diet supplements, and plastic surgery—that helped her escape prison or the hangman's noose. While her beauty certainly helped, there was also an intangible quality about her that comes across even now, more than a century later. She was bright and well educated; she played piano and could sing. But her greatest talent was in knowing how to enchant rich and powerful men. Her inner workings seemed inscrutable to the people who knew her when she lived, and she remains that way today. She partied with courtesans and the men who frequented their soirees, but she never was considered of their lower-class ilk. She most likely murdered and definitely blackmailed, committed forgery and fraud, stole, and manipulated. Her plots were complex and besides murder involved forged wills, bonds and stocks, raiding her lover's safe deposit box as he lay dying, an attempted incineration of her stepdaughter and then an effort to implicate her in the murder of her own father, and impersonation (her butler, heavily disguised, stood in as groom for her second wedding ceremony).

She was always cool, calm, and unfazed. "Nerve," "The Little Lady a Brick," "But She Stands a Cross-Fire without Shrinking" ran the bold headlines about Minnie's composure. Even when, at age sixteen, she was widowed, charged with murder, and forced to testify in court in front of hostile crowds, the convent-schooled girl never lost her composure. (Yes, it's true. Our Minnie studied with both the Ursuline nuns and the sisters at the St. Louis Institute in New Orleans. Oh, those poor nuns—though they taught her to write and read, they certainly had little impact on her soul.)

Indeed, she seemed so confident, her bearing so erect and her demeanor such that even though her testimony was a mishmash of half-truths, evasions, and outrageous lies, she never betrayed anxiousness, nor did she ever seem to entertain the thought the jury might find her guilty. Whereas even the innocent (and maybe she was but, come on, what are the odds?) might quail before prosecutors eager to convict, Minnie just sashayed through those inquests and courtrooms, taking her place in the witness box dressed in the latest and most fashionable of styles and composedly answered their harsh and demanding questions. She often turned her head to look directly at the jury when responding, making sure to meet their eyes and, oh, did those jurymen love that. Husbands left their wives and abandoned their families for her. No matter the destruction she left behind, the only pains she ever mentioned in the countless stories about her were the death of her mother and the loss of her mysterious third husband, Keating, the dashing British captain who might never have existed.

"She appeared as composed as if she had no connection with the case," wrote one newspaper reporter on October 23, 1885, as numerous druggists testified about her purchases of arsenic and store clerks told about her spending thousands a day. Then, it was her turn to testify. We'll let the court reporters tell that story.

She Made the Jurymen Weep
The (New York) World News, Wednesday 17, 1897

The climax of the case was reached when Mrs. Walkup was placed on the stand. Before she finished giving testimony the lawyers, jurymen and judge wept, and the stenographer's eyes were blinded so that he could not see to write.

The girl who had been befriended only by one man had captured the hearts of all, and they were ready to swear that she was innocent of the crime laid at her door. A verdict of acquittal was returned.

It wouldn't be the last time Minnie worked her wiles to escape the clutches of the law, and it probably wasn't the first.

1

TRUE LOVE NEVER RUNS SMOOTH

The Death of a New Groom

He died very suddenly. I am in trouble, as you will see by morning dispatches. Mrs. J. R. Walkup.

Those were the words Elizabeth Wallace read when she opened the telegram delivered to 222 Canal Street, her home in the French Quarter of New Orleans.

Mrs. J. R. Walkup was the name of her sixteen-year-old daughter, who had, exactly one month to the day previous, married James R. Walkup, a successful politician and businessman almost forty years her senior. But why would Minnie send such a formal missive from their home in Emporia, Kansas, and what type of trouble could she be in?

Big trouble as it turned out. In fact, she was in trouble even before Walkup, the one-time mayor of Emporia, had died.

The mysterious sudden illness and death of Hon. J. R. Walkup has been attended with most intense excitement in Emporia. Knots of agitated citizens during all of Friday night and Saturday morning discussed the event on the streets, as evidence of foul play on the part of his wife increased. A guard was mounted upon the residence and grounds. They patrolled the premises during the early morning hours of Saturday to prevent the escape of the young and beautiful woman who was suspected of the murder of the man to whom, less than a month ago, she had been married.

Visitors were generally prohibited access to the chamber of the rapidly sinking man. At 9 o'clock this morning strong hopes of his recovery were abandoned, his face grew ashen gray with the pallor of death, his breathing was heavy and he gasped for breath. The young wife was in the room. She caressed the dying man with the greatest apparent tenderness, kissing his lips and forehead passionately and imploring him to say if he knew her. His death at 10:45 this morning increased, if possible, the public excitement, and little else than this was thought of and talked of by the citizens. Newspaper extras were issued and sold in enormous numbers.

A post mortem examination of the remains was held this afternoon by Drs. Moore, Jacobs, Page, Harrison and Foncannon, and the stomach and intestines were found in a congested state with indications of corrosive poison. At 2 o'clock the coroner summoned a jury at the Walkup residence, and the taking of testimony was proceeded with.

A boy named William D. Willis, a second cousin of Mrs. Wallace, who about three weeks ago arrived here from New Orleans, has been also arrested and locked up. The boy was very angry, and said that he had stolen nothing, and did not see why he should be put in jail.

That this young and beautiful woman should thus, Borgia like, smite and slay her husband in the honeymoon in their life seems incredible. While it is true that suspicion rests strongly on her as to having administered the poison, yet it is not conclusive that she is responsible for his death. Our citizens will exercise toward her that charity and justice which is due to a woman so suddenly placed under such trying circumstances, away from parents and relatives, and among strangers.

The witnesses didn't paint a sympathetic portrait of Mrs. Wallace's beauteous belle of a daughter.

"Messrs. Ryder, M. H. Bates, and R. R. Kelly, druggists, testified that Mrs. Walkup had purchased arsenic at their respective stores," reported the *Times-Picayune*. "It was testified also that she had entire charge of the patient during his last sickness, administering all the medicine, etc. The Coroner at 4:30 this evening adjourned the jury and instructed the Sheriff to hold Mrs. Walkup in custody until Monday morning at 8 o'clock when the jury will meet again."

Also in custody was Minnie's cousin William (called Willie) Willis who had moved to Emporia about three weeks earlier and been warmly welcomed by not only Minnie but also her husband, who gave Willie a job and promised to send him to school. Willie had been orphaned years ago and raised by his great-aunt Elizabeth Wallace, making him more like Minnie's brother than a distant relative.

Minnie Wallace

A Beautiful New Orleans Bride of a Month,
Among Strangers in a Strange Land.
An Arrest for Causing the Death of Her Husband by Poison.
Times-Picayune, Sunday, August 23, 1885

Described by one news account as a fine specimen of a man and a Virginian gentleman, James Walkup was a Civil War veteran from West Virginia who made money in lumber and coal mines before moving to a farm northwest of Emporia in 1867. Thirteen years later, he and his family moved to Emporia, where he was active in politics and also worked the road taxes for the Santa Fe and other railroads in Kansas. The lucrative job entailed figuring out the taxes along the railroad routes that touched public highways. Always enterprising, Walkup opened a grocery store the year before his marriage to Minnie and was also involved in the coal trade. At the time of his death, he was serving his second term on the city council. He'd also recently been appointed by Governor Martin (whose son, in an interesting twist of fate, would marry Walkup's daughter Libbie) as a delegate to the River Improvement Convention in St. Paul, Minnesota.

In other words, James Walkup was a powerful, well connected, and successful businessman who fell in love (or lust) with the wrong woman—or rather, girl.

About fifty-two when he met Minnie (there are conflicting documents giving his birth year), he was a big man at six feet two inches and over two hundred pounds. His eyes were blue, his hair light brown, and he sported a small mustache. He and his daughters lived in a grand home at the corner of Merchant Street and Eleventh Avenue.

But despite his success and friendly personality, there were rumors of a dark side as well.

Twice widowed, Walkup was the father of three children, all older than the fifteen-year-old Minnie. Annie, his first wife, died giving birth to Walkup's oldest child and only son after just one year of marriage. A year later, Walkup married Hannah Maddock, and the couple had two daughters—Martha, born in 1861 and nicknamed Mattie and, five years later, Elizabeth Ann, or Libbie. Hannah was only forty-three when she died in 1884. Gossips passed around stories that Walkup had been neither a devoted nor an exceedingly kind husband to his second wife, and speculation abounded he'd worked her to death doing the cooking and cleaning for his various businesses.

Walkup drank, often to excess, and consorted with fast women and not just when he was single. In those pre-penicillin days, he very well could have been a cesspool of venereal disease, as would later be alleged at trial. Minnie later claimed he'd had a long-term relationship with Mary Moss, the African American woman live-in maid. What was his allure? Most likely his money—at least for Minnie and her mother, that was qualification enough.

When James Met Minnie

In December 1884, Walkup and his friend Eben Baldwin traveled by train to New Orleans to attend the New Orleans World's Industrial and Cotton Centennial Exposition. At the time the expo took place, almost one-third of the cotton grown in the United States was handled in New Orleans, the home of the Cotton Exchange. The event encompassed 249 acres from St.

Charles Avenue to the Mississippi River and was accessible not only by railway and horse and carriage but also via steamboats and oceangoing vessels. At 33 acres, the expo's main building was the largest roofed structure ever constructed up until then. Five thousand electric lights illuminated the expo, more than ten times the number existing in the city beyond the fairgrounds. The observation tower featured electric elevators and working models of experimental electric streetcars.

Other spectacles were the Horticultural Hall, the largest greenhouse in the world, and an octagonal-shaped building that housed the very popular Mexican exhibit, constructed at a cost of $200,000, where a large brass band played.

The expo was so popular that from its opening on December 16 to its closing in May 1885, more than one million people attended, including approximately thirty-six thousand the week of Mardi Gras. In typical New Orleans fashion, corruption ran rampant, and despite the huge attendance, the expo ended up losing a ton of money, most finding its way into politicians' over-large pockets.

It appears that for Baldwin, attending the expo was the number-one reason for going to New Orleans. Walkup's agenda instead focused more on fun and included visiting the city's bordellos. The famed red-light district known as Storyville wasn't in existence at the time, but the city certainly offered lots of options for men desiring to indulge their vices. Accordingly, by the laws of supply and demand, the number of working girls increased exponentially as well. Mrs. Wallace's boardinghouse in the lively French Quarter had been recommended to the two men as a place to stay.

Elizabeth Wallace, a divorcée, and her beautiful daughters, of whom Minnie was the acknowledged loveliest, were part of the package for those staying at 222 Canal Street. Minnie, with her convent school education, played piano, and Dora, who by then was married to a penniless artist named Edward Findlay, sang in accompaniment. It was a pretty picture, but Walkup's interest was neither cultural nor paternal. On the morning after first meeting her youngest daughter, Walkup told Elizabeth he wanted to marry Minnie.

How pretty was Minnie? Based on the hundreds of newspaper articles, the decision appears unanimous. She was amazingly lovely. Here is a typical description: "Miss Minnie is a tall, graceful, slender but well-developed girl with perfect complexion, white, with the roses blooming on her cheeks blood red. Her hair is long and black, and large black eyes and heavy eyelashes, with a mastery of expression, complete the picture, which is a rare one. She was noted for her beauty, which early on had many admirers."

No one, and I mean no one, ever wrote a negative word about her looks even as she entered her forties.

Elizabeth wasn't impressed with Walkup, who was drunk day and night. Baldwin wasn't happy about his friend's infatuation either, afraid that he might succeed in making Minnie his wife. Not shutting the door entirely on the romance, when it came time for the men to leave and Walkup asked for permission to write to Minnie, Elizabeth agreed.

Returning to rock-solid Kansas didn't cool Walkup's ardor, and he wrote to her renewing his offer of marriage. Minnie had just turned sixteen.

In early spring, Walkup, accompanied by his youngest daughter and a family friend, returned to New Orleans. The expo was still going on, and Walkup and his daughter Libbie, along with Minnie and her family, attended together. Still hopelessly infatuated, Walkup offered Elizabeth $4,000 if she would give permission for Minnie to marry him. That amount equals about $100,000 in today's money. Elizabeth would later claim that she turned him down, saying it was up to Minnie whether she wanted to marry him.

But before lauding Elizabeth's mothering skills, keep this in mind: she was a serial prevaricator and told this story only after Walkup's death as a way to counter criticism about how she had encouraged Minnie to marry Walkup to get his fortune. The press, though, always awed by Minnie's beauty, usually took the side of the men who fell into her clutches, seeing them as powerless to withstand her wiles.

> The beauty and the charms of Minnie increased in about the same proportion that rumors of her frailty spread and men were attracted around her like moths round a candle. Staid lawyers, learned judges, sagacious businessmen, flippant fops, and conceited dudes alike did homage at her shrine; she reigned a veritable queen among them, the admired of all.
>
> Then the exposition brought strangers to add to the worshippers, and among them came J.R. Walkup, of Emporia, Kansas, a well-to-do elderly gentleman with grown daughters. He joined the other moths, fluttered around round the candle and was scorched. He fell a victim, a helpless captive at her feet, and then came the sad sequel. He carried her off, announced to the world he had married her (although the same suspicion and mystery surrounded that ceremony as surrounded all other events with which this affair is connected), and brought her into the bosom of his family against their will, and against the advice and protestations of his friends.
>
> Today he is in his grave, the victim, as is charged of poison, administered for whom he braved all, sacrificed everything, and who, having enamored him into her power, ruthlessly removed him out of the way, it is supposed.
>
> —*Topeka Daily Capital*, Tuesday, September 8, 1885

The word *fragility* in the above paragraph most likely implies Minnie surrendered her "charms," if given the right inducement. The takeaway is that poor James, having no choice, was not the pursuer but the victim here.

Oh, give us a break.

If Walkup made the offer and was turned down, as Elizabeth claimed, it didn't discourage him. Instead, he upped the ante. He promised a job to Willie and to send him to school. As for Edward, who certainly wasn't making a success of his portrait painting business, if he and Dora moved to Emporia, he'd give him a job as well. When all was finally settled, Walkup kept his bargain—he sent for Willie. Unfortunately, before Willie could make much of the offers, Walkup would be dead.

By the time Walkup returned in May, Minnie was seriously considering his offer and a tentative date had been set. But first, the Wallace women traveled to Emporia to see if he was as wealthy as he claimed. The trip was a success as far as all were concerned. Minnie would become his wife.

If it all seems coldhearted (and believe me, as you continue with Minnie's story you'll find she made glaciers seem like soft-serve ice cream), marrying for money was a fair exchange—her extreme youth and stunning beauty in exchange for his fortune.

Let us stop here and give James Walkup his due. Though Minnie was fifteen when they met, when she was on trial less than a year later, one of the jurors said they found it hard to believe she wasn't twenty-three or so. So maybe he wasn't a cradle robber—or not as much of one.

Interestingly, although in today's world we are more accepting—and rightly so—of so many things that would have been illegal back then such as biracial and same sex marriages, society has become less accepting of extreme age differences; a fifteen-year-old girl being courted by a fifty-plus-year-old man would be considered seriously creepy and most likely lead to charges of child abuse. Not back then. Marriage was often conducted like a business and understood as such.

The Ultimate Bridezilla
Saint Paul Globe, Tuesday, August 25, 1885

On July 7 last Mrs. Wallace determined upon a visit to a sick sister at Covington, Kentucky, and took Miss Minnie along. They found Mr. Walkup there, he being also on a visit to relatives. When the engaged couple met they decided that there was no reason for delaying the ceremony until October. So instead of being married at New Orleans in October they were married at Covington in July.

The wedding took place July 22 and was a brilliant affair. There were some sixty persons present. Dr. Laer, a Methodist minister, performed the ceremony. The bride never looked more charming, and, in an elegant costume of blue silk and white lace, was the admiration of all beholders. The entire party crossed over the river to Cincinnati and a fine supper was served at a residence of a relative, Mrs. Moore, on Plum Street. Mrs. Wallace bid them goodbye at Cincinnati and returned to New Orleans a few days later.

The bridal couple seemed very happy and left for Niagara Falls, making a short trip and then going direct to the home of the groom in Emporia, Kans.

They reached there about two weeks ago, and their arrival created a sensation. The fame of Miss Minnie's beauty had preceded her, and this, added to Mr. Walkup's popularity, insured her a glorious welcome. They were met at the depot by a large gathering, escorted to their home by the Knights of Pythias band, and held a reception in the evening. The Council called in a body and the members tendered their congratulations. They mayor gave them a reception and formally introduced Mrs. Walkup into Emporia society.

She wrote home that there had never been such excitement in Emporia since the Mayor's wedding four years ago. About the time of their arrival Miss Libbie Walkup left home on a short visit to Denver, but has since returned. Mr. Walkup acted as mayor a short while during the latter's absence.

From her letters it seemed as if Minnie was living as happy as a bird with her mate in a cozy situation with no wants unprovided. Her last letter, received five days ago, said that Mr. Walkup was going on a short trip on business and that she was to go along. Mr. Walkup wrote in the same strain. Mrs. Wallace heard no more from them until yesterday, when she received the news of her son-in-law's death, and she did not believe in the truth of the intelligence.

Somehow both Elizabeth and Minnie had forgotten to tell her father or close family friend Judge Houston about marrying Mr. Walkup. James Wallace believed his daughter and ex-wife were visiting relatives in Missouri. What Judge Houston thought, we don't know. But both learned of marriage—and the groom's death—when they read it in the newspaper.

As for James Walkup, if he had paid more attention, he might have seen that all was not perfect in his marriage.

Practice Makes Perfect? The Case of the Arsenic-Laced Beer
Mrs. Wallace Walkup Sued
She Is Now Accused of Having Poisoned an Emporia Man.
Emporia Daily News, Tuesday, August 25, 1885

William Born, a beef packer of Emporia Kansas has come to
Topeka to file in the Federal Court suit for $10,000 damages
against Mrs. Minnie Wallace Walkup, who asserts she is the
widow of J.R. Ketchum [*sic*]. The suit will revive Mrs. Ketcham's
history as a sensational character.

A few weeks after her marriage to Mayor Walkup, he invited
some gentlemen, among them Mr. Born, to spend the evening
at his home. While they were there Mr. Walkup asked his wife
to serve some beer. She opened the bottles in the kitchen and
returned with filled glasses, which she handed around.

Born asserts that he drained his glasses immediately,
but Walkup set his own glass on the table and continued the
conversation.

Born then alleged that Walkup shoved his filled glass toward
him, insisting he drink it. So, he did, and shortly afterward,
he was seized with convulsions and began vomiting a yellow-
ish-green substance. Lingering for months near death, he was
diagnosed as suffering from the effects of arsenic poisoning. He
believed that Minnie had put poison in the glass Walkup had
given him, as Born claimed he drank only four glasses of beer
and ate nothing at the gathering.

Born timed his lawsuit after the Walkup estate had finally
been settled, explaining he did so "now that she has money."

Poison in the Beer

A Sequel to the Strange Case at Emporia Kansas
One of The Guests at The Walkup Wedding Believes He
Got Hold of a Glass of Beer Intended for Someone Else
Delaware County Daily Times (Chester,
Pennsylvania), Thursday, August 27, 1885

Born was a longtime friend of Walkup and, according to Dr.
L. D. Jacobs, who also treated Mr. Walkup during his last illness,
their symptoms were almost identical—though Born had the
good fortune to survive.

"I have never experienced such feeling before," Born told a reporter. He then hesitated and added, "I believe I got the wrong glass of beer."

Added weight was given to Born's theory when it was discovered that a few days after her arrival in Emporia, Minnie took a white powder that she'd purchased in Cincinnati to an Emporia druggist and asked him to analyze it for arsenic.

Baby, Baby Where Did Our Love Go?

Like he had promised before their marriage, Walkup had Willie Willis move to Emporia with the intention of sending him to school and helping him establish a successful career.

Willie Willis was eleven months older than Minnie. His mother, a niece of Mrs. Wallace, died of consumption when he was three years old and left him in Elizabeth's care. He didn't remember his father, John D. Willis, who had died in Florida several years earlier. Whether his father had remarried, giving him half siblings, Willie didn't know. It all painted a rather sad picture of a boy abandoned twice: once by the death of his mother and then emotionally and physically by his father.

Willie—a delicate boy of slender build, with a pale face, blue eyes, and light hair—was described by some who knew him as a friendly, likeable child—a good kid with a playful disposition; others said he exhibited confirmed bad habits and a vicious character. He also showed symptoms of the consumption that killed his mother.

As for Minnie, though Walkup stated she seemed happy and satisfied, let's face it—he had no idea. After all, she was most likely already planning on poisoning him. Minnie was just a kid, and though obviously she liked the idea of being a rich man's wife, she probably didn't like the job requirements that went with it.

Mr. Walkup was happy, though, writing a letter to Mrs. Wallace nine days before his death:

> Topeka, Kans., August 13, 1885.—I avail myself of writing you
> a few lines. I came here to-day on business with the railroad

company. Will go back to-morrow. Minnie has written to you three times a week since we arrived at home. Willie arrived all right and is delighted with the city and country. He has written to you since he came. He is going to start school next month. I want him to go nine months steady. Minnie is perfectly satisfied. She appears to be as well satisfied as if she was at home at New Orleans, and you may rest assured that I will leave nothing undone to make her happy. We are going next week to Omaha, Nebraska, for a few days. I have not been away from home but one day since we were married. You may rest assured that Minnie is well contented and happy. Thanking you for giving me as good and affectionate wife as Minnie is, I will close. Yours truly, J. R. Walkup

So what led Minnie to murder, and when did she decide to do so?

If Born was accidentally poisoned just two weeks after James and Minnie's nuptials, what happened to turn their marriage deadly so quickly? Even if Minnie didn't spike the beer with arsenic (but then how else did it get in there?), she surely did poison James two weeks later.

One surmise, put forward by newspaper reporters, was Walkup wasn't going to let his sixteen-year-old wife fritter his fortune away. He treated Minnie like a beautiful ornamental doll, misjudging her character and not comprehending that she might be thinking he hadn't kept up his side of the bargain. After all, fair is fair. There is another portent Walkup missed. Not only did Minnie hit the stores like a hurricane, buying a prodigious number of items, but she was also shipping them to New Orleans.

Was she stocking up because she planned on divorcing him? We wish we could ask her. But all we can do is report what the newspapers and court testimony tell us.

The Shopaholic

Minnie was not a beauty who downplayed her looks. She loved beautiful clothes and spent much of her time shopping. One of the stores she frequented was the elite Newman & Co., where clerks Eunice Bartlett and Maggie J. Evans often waited on her. Both became witnesses for the prosecution.

On the stand, Eunice recalled a conversation on August 10 where Minnie inquired about the price of some silk and then asked when her husband settled his accounts. Bartlett said the bill was presented on the first of each month. Realizing she had several weeks before he'd learn about any purchases she'd made in August, Minnie bought between $60 and $80 (between $1,440 and $1,900 today) worth of goods.

Not too long after that, said Maggie Evans, Minnie had made purchases totaling $100 ($2,400) and charged them to Mr. Walkup's account.

Minnie took much of what she brought (as well as some of Libbie's clothing) to the Wells Fargo office and shipped them to her mother's home. More baffling, in at least one case, she sent some purchases to St. Louis. Walkup, discovering what she was doing, grabbed a hatchet and headed down to the Wells Fargo office, where he hacked open one of her boxes.

We have questions, and Walkup should have, too. Why ship all these clothes, as well as other household items, back to New Orleans when she lived in Emporia? And why wasn't Minnie worried about the bill coming due in September? Was it because she knew Walkup would be in no position to complain by then?

Minnie thought she was marrying a rich man who would indulge all of her whims, but life in Emporia (a nice little city but nothing like New Orleans) with a stingy man—or even worse, one who really didn't have all that much money—wasn't what she'd signed on for.

L. M. Carter, an acquaintance of Minnie's, recalled a conversation he had with her about a week after Walkup's death.

"Mrs. Walkup told me that evening she supposed Mr. Walkup to be well off when he died," Carter testified in court, "but since Walkup's death she had discovered there was a mortgage on everything."

Another reason, we think, that Walkup's time on earth was quickly coming to a close.

Back Home on Canal Street

When Minnie's telegram arrived, Dora was about to give birth to her first child. Edward doesn't seem to have been torn about whether to stay with his wife to see her safely through delivery—remember this was a time when one out of every three women died in childbirth—or to rush to the side of his incomparable sister-in-law.

Within fifteen minutes or so, he was off to catch a train to Emporia. Elizabeth, who was ill, would also journey north later. Judge Houston, who was vacationing in Long Branch, New Jersey, quickly headed to Emporia as he heard the news

As word spread that a New Orleans girl was suspected of murdering her husband, reporters hurried to the Wallace home. Elizabeth told them about receiving the telegram that afternoon. Because it was signed "Mrs. J. R. Walkup," she at first hadn't thought it was really from Minnie, who typically signed her first name when writing to her mother.

Elizabeth had even more cause for worry when the reporters told her Minnie was a suspect in Walkup's death. The Wallace women were always gracious and willing to talk to reporters no matter the situation, which is one reason reporters, for the most part, wrote so favorably about them. Confronted with these tidings, Elizabeth didn't become hysterical but instead maintained her composure and expressed her deep sorrow for her daughter, a bride of just one month and now a widow far from home.

At midnight, more news arrived from Emporia, and reporters, who either were camping out at the Canal Street house or felt comfortable arriving back at her door late at night, updated Elizabeth on what was happening. Willie had been arrested and taken to jail, they said, and Minnie was under guard in her house.

Elizabeth, emphasizing her belief in their innocence, said neither Minnie nor Willie had any motive and that neither was capable of such an action. The mystery would be cleared up, she avowed.

Minnie married Mr. Walkup because she loved him, continued Elizabeth, adding that she had warned Walkup that her daughter was too young to marry. She'd also pointed out to the besotted old goat that his daughters would be upset by the match. Walkup, showing his deep fatherly instincts, told Elizabeth that if they objected he'd cut them off without a cent—always a good way to help foster positive relationships between children and a new stepparent.

At the time of this discussion, Walkup and his daughter Libbie were in New Orleans. For that short period, Libbie and Minnie seemed close. Of course, all rapidly changed after the marriage. Mattie, his oldest daughter, opposed the marriage from the beginning.

Champions to a Woman in Distress

Though Minnie paints herself as being alone and friendless, before long a plethora of wealthy elderly men, as well as her penurious older brother-in-law, surrounded her, offering both financial and emotional aid. None seemed to worry that what had befallen one man could just as easily happen to them. But then, though it might be trite, is there any truer truism than there's no fool like an old fool? In Minnie's case, the answer was no.

First let's eliminate the brother-in-law's possibilities. No matter how attentive and gallant he might have been, Edward Findlay never had a chance—he was too poor.

After meeting with Minnie, Edward told reporters she was very cheerful. He also talked about a poisoning case he'd heard about where a man died after drinking arsenic-laced coffee. People thought he had been murdered, was the gist of Edward's story, but it turned out that arsenic used by paper hangers had accidentally fallen into a coffee mill and then ultimately into the cup of coffee the man drank. Nice try, Edward.

Judge Houston, who had known Minnie since she was a baby, traveled to Emporia immediately upon hearing the news. A stranger also arrived on the scene.

The Honorable William Jay, a sixty-year-old Emporia lumber merchant, was a married man of wealth and influence and highly regarded in the community. Shortly before the trial was to begin, Jay saw a picture of Minnie in the newspaper and, reading innocence in her eyes, determined to help her no matter the cost.

"He who giveth to the poor lendeth to the Lord," Jay said. Despite quoting a Bible verse, Jay wanted people to know he was not a church member, thank you, and had no religion outside of giving support to sick and helping the needy and the afflicted. To him that meant Minnie. One does wonder if she hadn't been so beautiful whether he would have been better able to see the guilt that must have been in her eyes.

Jail Time, Minnie Style: No Hard Time for Her
Mrs. Walkup in Jail.
Evidence Against Her Gaining Strength—Visited by Her Mother
New York Times, August 29, 1885

There was the sound of wheels this afternoon in front of the residence of Mrs. Minnie Walkup, who is under arrest on the charge of poisoning her husband, and the Sheriff, who was in the house, went down and opened the door.

Minnie's mother arrived at the Walkup home just as Minnie was about to be taken to the courthouse, where a room had been prepared for her on the upper floor. Crying, the two women embraced before Minnie was taken away. In other words, house arrest was over and Minnie was on her way to jail.

This news brought more tears between mother and daughter, but Minnie soon got control of herself and calmly let herself be escorted to her new living quarters.

As soon as Minnie left her home, Mayor Hood, who had that day been appointed administrator of the Walkup estate, closed up the house immediately.

But Minnie wasn't subjected to hard jail time. Instead of being behind bars, Minnie ate with the sheriff's wife and children and was treated as a member of their family, remaining with them in their rooms instead of being confined to her own.

Nor was the room where Minnie stayed stark and cold. It was, as most jail cells aren't, carpeted, well furnished, and comfortable. There was an organ in the sheriff's home, and when young ladies stopped by to visit Minnie, they all played and sang. The crowds of visitors were at times so large that some had to be turned away. Minnie also left the confines of the jail, going on rides with the sheriff and his wife in their hack.

In other words, Minnie's incarceration was like a long and pleasurable stay with friends.

About the time Minnie was housed in the sheriff's residence, Willie, who really had been in jail, was released. No charges were ever filed against him, but because he was a witness, he remained in town and felt free to express his indignation about being arrested.

Years later, Minnie gave her side of the story in an article she wrote for the Sunday, December 26, 1897, edition of the *Chicago Daily Tribune*.

> One month after my marriage my husband died––His physician said from arsenical poisoning. I was accused by his children of having murdered him.
>
> I had just passed 16 and had no one in the whole state of Kansas to turn to for word of comfort and advice. I was arrested, and my mother came from New Orleans to me at once. My mother had little money and I felt that the whole world was against me, that I was the cynosure of all eyes and the first two or three days they were sharp and unfriendly eyes.
>
> At last people commenced to ask if it was possible that a girl whose first long dress was her wedding dress, whose face was childish, could be the Lucretia Borgia her enemies were painting her. One man came forward and said: "from this time to take up her cause and spend my money and my time in her defense."
>
> He employed lawyers to defend me and gave me the protection that I only hope God in his infinite wisdom will someday give me the chance to offer some friendless girl. Mr. William Jay, my Abou Ben Achem, as I grew to call him, defended and brought people to look at both sides of the case.

Elizabeth soon had her hands full managing all the strong personality types surrounding Minnie (excluding poor, hapless

Edward). Often described as a "woman of business" when it came to negotiating for her daughters, she wanted cash, not council, to pay for Minnie's legal defense. Judge Houston, considered one of the most corrupt of New Orleans' politicians—which was no small feat—wasn't about to spend his ill-gotten gains easily. The romantic Jay announced he would stand by Minnie as long as he had a dollar, a pointed dig at Houston.

Jay recommended, given Minnie's youth, that she be appointed a guardian—him. Houston argued Minnie's marriage meant she was emancipated, and he wanted to be her administrator. Elizabeth was afraid that Houston might persuade Minnie to marry him. But why?

Long-simmering rumors had it that Houston had been the lover of Elizabeth, then Dora and now Minnie.

Others whispered Houston was Minnie's father. James Wallace, Minnie's putative father and now pretty much an incompetent drunk, told reporters he didn't known if Minnie was his biological daughter. When Minnie was born, Judge Houston served as her godfather. When Elizabeth filed for divorce, Judge Houston granted it. Could it be that unbeknownst to Houston, Minnie was his daughter? Seems farfetched, like a very bad soap opera or overwrought Gothic novel. But actually, bad soap opera is a good summation of the Wallace family saga.

Elizabeth asked Houston what he was going to do for Minnie. He said he was waiting to see what Elizabeth did but that if he was in her place and his daughter's life was at stake, he would sell all his jewelry and even his furniture to save her. Elizabeth wasn't about to do that it seems.

Wallace, whom one reporter described as having "sharp claws beneath a dawny demeanor," questioned why Houston was even there then.

Houston replied that as Minnie's godfather, he was next to her father in the line of authority to protect her. Elizabeth retorted that he could best act like the father's part by providing money instead of sitting around and giving out advice. In the end, handing over money wasn't part of Houston's game plan.

Exit Judge Houston, who returned to the East Coast where he'd been vacationing.

Money aside, Elizabeth thought Minnie should have a local person of good standing as her guardian, giving her not only a home court advantage but emphasizing her youth. Mr. Jay with his property and popularity was just the ticket.

So, the sixty-year-old Jay applied and was appointed guardian by the judge. Under the terms of the guardianship, any money he spent on her was to be refunded from Minnie's share of the Walkup estate. Of course, there were risks, the most obvious being Minnie might be found guilty and would hang instead of becoming a beneficiary of the will. There was also the question of how much she would inherit even if found innocent. The final and most concerning question—due to its likelihood for those of us who know Minnie best—was if she were acquitted and awarded her inheritance, what were the chances she'd repay even one cent of any money Jay spent in her defense before leaving town?

Jay, believing he was saving a damsel in distress, spent more than $4,000 of his own money on her defense—almost $100,000 today. His unwavering support of Minnie was priceless, turning public sentiment in her favor. Many called at the house to wish her well, and she received an abundance of bouquets and floral arrangements. One magnificent basket of flowers was accompanied by a card reading, "From the ladies of Emporia, who recognize your noble qualities and believe in your innocence." Check with us at the end of the trial for an update on that sentiment. But here's a clue: they should have saved their money, as they would soon find out.

Meanwhile back in New Orleans, Dora Findlay gave birth to an infant daughter she named Minnie Wallace Findlay. What she thought of her husband being with her sister and not with her, we can only guess.

On September 7, Elizabeth returned to New Orleans and by the next day was chatting with a reporter from the *Times-Picayune*. She had a story to sell: Walkup was a scoundrel who was a horrid husband to her dear, sweet, and naïve daughter.

"I always liked Mr. Walkup, but I am astonished at what has come out about him at Emporia since his death," said Elizabeth. "His mother says that Minnie was Walkup's third wife. His first wife was a beautiful woman and lived a little over a year. His second wife is reported not have been treated the best in the world. From the testimony of the physicians and others Walkup had been using arsenic for eight to ten years. He probably told Minnie to buy some for him. Minnie says nothing except that she is innocent."

Elizabeth went on, telling the reporter how everyone in Emporia was on Minnie's side, and then went after Libbie Walkup.

> "When I first saw Miss Libbie, Walkup's daughter, after reaching Emporia, she threw her arms around my neck and kissed me. Afterwards I heard that she had spread the reports that a letter had been received from me, telling Minnie to get Walkup out of the way before October. Of course, I never wrote such a letter."
>
> Minnie's lawyer has called upon Libbie to produce the letter and she said that it was gone. Another time she said that she had seen it but could not find it.

This wasn't the first time the Wallaces had put forth the idea that Libbie and her siblings helped engineer Minnie's arrest to keep her from inheriting. During her interview with the reporter, Elizabeth also suggested that Mary Moss had disappeared and a warrant was out for her arrest. Moss hadn't skipped town and would later testify Minnie had asked her to say she was buying butter when she actually was trying to buy arsenic.

As a public relations team spewing insinuations, the Wallaces were hard to beat. Elizabeth had one last parting shot to tell the female reporter.

"Libbie has never worn mourning for her father yet," she said.

2

THERE IS A HOUSE IN
NEW ORLEANS

Mrs. Minnie Wallace Walker Ketchum's [*sic*] Own
Pathetic Story of Her Exciting Career
She Asserts She Is Not by Any Means the
Lucretia Borgia Her Enemies Paint Her,
Compares Herself to Dumas' Camille
Chicago Daily Tribune, Sunday, December 26, 1897

It is a test indeed to write this story: the woman with a "past"
is so often one without a future, that it is difficult situation to
express and my unfortunate past dates back to the earliest days
of my girlhood so that life for me has not always been filled with
sunshine. In view of the many untruthful exaggerated accounts
of those unhappy days that are current in the papers, it is only
justice to myself and to those friends who have ever stood ready
to assist and defend me to state the facts as they occurred. It is
unnecessary to dwell upon my recent bereavement for the papers
have made those most private and sacred affairs of my life and
heart matters of comment.

I was born in New Orleans Jan. 14, 1869. My parents lived
in an aristocratic part of the city. I was fortunate enough to be
surrounded by people who were well bred and used to the nicer

things of life. Amid those surroundings I early acquired a taste for the refinements and elegancies. My childhood passed without event. I was educated at the St. Louis Institute and was a dreamy, quiet, bookish child. My childhood passed without event. At 15, I had gone home from the institute to spend vacation with my dear mother. Mister James Reeves Walkup, ex-mayor of Emporia Kansas visited New Orleans at this time and among his letters of introduction was one to my mother. He was welcomed as a guest at our house. It soon became apparent that he was in love with me. Of course, I did not love a man past 50 years of age with daughters and a son older than I. After visiting New Orleans for a while he went back to Emporia and returned soon after with his unmarried daughter.

He urged [and] his suit and was accepted. We were married July 22, 1885.

Let's stop right here in reading Minnie's piteous story and correct some, ahem, unpleasant facts that she seems to have, of course, inadvertently left out. But where to start unraveling the many falsehoods in her story?

Maybe the best way is to take what the contemporaneous news reports had to say about her early years.

There are so many mysteries surrounding the Wallace women, starting with Minnie's mother, Elizabeth. Her maiden name is commonly spelled Higgins in newspaper accounts, though at times it appears as Hagan. When she married James Wallace, her last name was not (and this will be important to note as we continue with her story) listed as Kirby—the name of her allegedly deceased former husband and the father of her daughter Dora Kirby, Minnie's older half sister—but as Egan on their wedding certificate. Higgins, Hagan, and Egan are all variations of the same name and one of them, most likely Egan, is the correct spelling.

Higgins/Hagan/Egan grew up on a farm in Ohio. She must have longed for something more than hard days in the field and, one day when riding atop the farm's produce as the horse and wagon made its way to market, she decided enough with farming and ran away to Cincinnati, where she met Dr. Patrick Kirby.

Whether they married or not depends on who was telling the story. Elizabeth claimed she and Kirby married across the Ohio River in Covington, Kentucky. At the time they were covering Minnie's trial, the *Topeka Daily Capital* searched for their marriage record but couldn't find it. I did the same only using much more effective search engines, such as Ancestry.com and FamilySearch, with the same lack of results.

Whatever her marital status—Elizabeth had a daughter whom she named Dora Kirby. Either with or without Kirby, Elizabeth ended up in New Orleans and, at some point, declared herself a widow. Here again, a search of documents fails to turn up a Patrick Kirby in New Orleans or Ohio that would fit with Elizabeth's narrative. Be that as it may, in the future, when Dora married (and she married at least twice), she would list her father as Patrick Kirby.

So Minnie, with her strength, cool poise, and infinite capabilities to work her way through extreme difficulties, wasn't an anomaly among the Wallace women. Described as "fair and sprightly," Elizabeth soon found a new husband—James Elijah Wallace, a successful attorney and a United States commissioner in New Orleans.

James, Elizabeth, and little Dora, by then about seven years old, lived first at 83 Rampart Street where their daughter, Minnie, was born on January 14, 1869. The family then moved to Draydes Street near Calliope and then to 44 Dauphine Street.

To hear Elizabeth tell it, James began drinking heavily, was abusive, and couldn't support his family, forcing her to let furnished rooms for boarders in order to pay the bills.

Here we again enter another contradictory part of Elizabeth's life. Did Elizabeth run just a simple boardinghouse, free of any hint of scandal? That's the story Elizabeth, Minnie, and Dora would have us believe. But if it were just a boardinghouse, why were so many prominent, older men frequent visitors? Surely, it wasn't just to hear Dora sing and Minnie play the piano.

James Wallace's depiction of life at 44 Dauphine Street differs. Growing suspicions about his wife's behavior, he discovered she was having an affair with one of the boarders. He also was growing tired of the "prolonged boisterous revelry" among both the boarders and the guests who frequented the house at all hours. That ended the marriage for him. Elizabeth's take? Wallace's cruelty, drunkenness, and lack of support forced her to file for a decree of separation, which she did in Judge Lynch's court in 1873. This was the initial stage in Elizabeth's attempt to get a divorce at a time when legally they were difficult to secure.

In 1875, Wallace filed for divorce. Then, worried about how the publicity would impact Minnie, he dropped his suit. Elizabeth had no such qualms and filed a divorce petition stating there was no chance of reconciliation. The civil court judge who signed the final decree of divorce was W. T. Houston, Minnie's godfather and frequent visitor at 44 Dauphine. Free of Wallace, Elizabeth moved her daughters to 27 Bourbon Street at the corner of Customhouse Street.

As the *Topeka Daily Capital* put it: "At No. 27 Bourbon the orgies of No. 44 Dauphine were kept up, and restauranteurs thereabout aver that the wealthiest and most valuable of their customers unaccountably found their way to the Wallace house, and after one visit the restaurants knew them no more."

Wallace claimed Elizabeth kept him from seeing Minnie, and sometime after the divorce, Elizabeth took it one step further, telling him Minnie wasn't his daughter and that her name was really Minnie Reynolds—which one newspaper said was the name she'd been enrolled with at school.

As for Judge Houston, he continued to be a presence in the new dwelling and is a prime example of how the Wallace women were able to forge bonds with older, successful, and so-willing-to-be helpful men.

Family Antecedents
Topeka Daily Capital, Tuesday, September 8, 1885

So far as we are concerned about the affair, knowing the character, history and antecedents of Minnie Reynolds, Wallace, Walkup or whatever name she is most entitled to bear, and her family history as we do, and in the light of the evidence transmitted over the wires from Emporia, Kansas, we feel no hesitation in saying that Mr. J.R. Walkup is only another victim of the fatal influence that attends this ill-omened family, and which it seems is destined to fall upon all who come within reach of their blighting touch—although we are not prepared to say now by whose hand he died.

The Wallace boarding house, operated by Mrs. Wallace, mother of Minnie, has been known to men-about-town for the last 12 years and up to within a few years, have been regarded as one of the questionable character to say the least, where politicians, gamblers and fast men were wont to gather and wine flowed freely to the sound of revelry and mirth, without much regard to restraint or constraint of speech or manner.

During the halcyon days of the Republican regime in this state more than one shining light of the "grand old party of mortality and virtue" passed his evenings and parted with his cash in the gilded parlors of No. 44 Dauphin and No. 27 Bourbon streets, the furnished rooms [at the] establishments of the Wallace family.

Amid the sports who lived in the home at this time were Charlie Crushers, alias "Handsome Charlie," Jim Rooley and others as well-known who are living to attest the truth of these statement.

It is probably coincidence that Judge Houston, an ultimate New Orleans political player who finally gave Elizabeth her freedom from an alcoholic downwardly mobile attorney, was also a good friend of the family. And we're sure that his particular interest in Dora, who, like all the Wallace girls, blossomed quickly, was of an avuncular rather than a sexual nature. After all, he was married and considerably older, though that didn't stop him from squiring Minnie's older sibling about town. Such attention continued even after a very pregnant Dora married the much older portrait painter Edward Findlay (at times spelled Finley) on April 19, 1879.

There was talk that Houston was the father of Dora's baby and her marriage to Findlay was a matter of convenience. What besides lack of choice, people asked, would make such a lovely young woman waste herself on an old man with poor prospects?

Now, we're willing to believe that Houston and Dora had a platonic relationship—think uncle and niece—but people will always talk and reporters will always write. And so they did. The *Mascot*, a kind of a counterculture newspaper described by the *Times-Picayune* as an "irreverent, pungent, scandal-mongering weekly," wrote about Houston's relationships with the Wallaces.

"The *Mascot* started off more as a political magazine but then they started getting into writing about scandals," says Sally Asher, an artist, writer, photographer, and blogger who has researched and written about the *Mascot* extensively. One of the *Mascot*'s satirical columns, Bridget Magee's Society Notes, was written in the heavy brogue of an Irish woman. The column poked fun at the city's politicians and social elite. In January 1885—about the time that Minnie was giving in to James Walkup's pleas to marry—"Bridget" wrote a scathing column on Houston, whom she called an "autocrat" and "would-be satrap." She also implied he and Dora were having an affair because she was seen with him at the Rex Ball (the extravagant concluding event of the Mardi Gras season).

Honor was all, even for rascals. When Judge Houston's hotheaded brother James, who was the state tax collector, read the story, he decided to horsewhip the *Mascot* editors. Supported by his friend Robert Brewster, the ex-sheriff and current Louisiana register of voters, the two walked into the *Mascot* offices. The outcome was not what they expected.

Sharp Shooting

A Brisk Fusillade in the Mascot Office.
Jas. D. Houston and Robert Brewster Go in to Give Its
Editor a Clubbing—They Make Their Way Out Wounded,
The Former in His Right Hand, the Latter
with Four Holes in His Body.
Brewster's Wounds Regarded as Fatal—George
Osmond, of the Mascot, also Wounded.
Times-Picayune, Tuesday, January 13, 1885

Camp Street at noon yesterday, as it was a very bright, pleasant day, was crowded with pedestrians, not a few of whom were ladies and children. The usual bustle of business was interrupted by three reports in quick succession in the vicinity of Commercial Alley. The reports, although not loud, were yet sufficient to attract everyone within hearing and heads were turned hither and thither in the effort to discover whence proceeded the ominous sounds.

Not many seconds elapsed ere other and sharper reports followed and soon all eyes were concentrated on the third-story windows of the Mascot office from whence the noise appeared to come.

Some few seconds elapsed when, suddenly, two men appeared at the Camp Street door of the Mascot office and while one of them advanced to the middle of Camp Street, the other proceeded up Camp toward Natchez Street. The one who appeared in the street was Mr. James D. Houston and the other was Mr. Robert Brewster, Register of Voters, and both had been wounded the latter quite seriously.

Mr. Houston stood in the street looking up at the office of the Mascot, then turned, crossed the street to Mr. Hyatt's stationary [sic] store, which he entered. Mr. Brewster proceeded up Camp Street to the corner of Natchez, where he entered the Metropolitan Bank and seated himself on a chair, almost fainting, from pain and loss of blood.

These two participants in the shooting had scarcely disappeared from the sight of the bystanders ere another man appeared at the door of the Mascot office. This was Mr. George Ormond, one the proprietors and editor of the paper who was also wounded. He blew a police whistle and brought Office Early to the scene and him he surrendered. He requested the officer to conduct him to Mr. I.L. Kyoner's drug store, corner of Camp and Gravier streets to have his wounds dressed.

Eventually all four men, including the unarmed *Mascot* employee Adolph Zennecke, who defended himself by throwing an iron stove cover (which hit its mark), found themselves at Central Station, though Brewster, whose wounds were the most serious, was then sent on to the Charity Hospital. One bullet had entered his chest near his heart, producing a life-threatening wound. Another bullet had grazed his thigh, one entered his right forearm, and the last hit above his right elbow. In Ward No. 14, Brewster was sedated with opiates and by 5:00 p.m. on the day of the shooting was said to be resting easily. That wouldn't last.

So, what on earth happened on the third floor of the *Mascot*'s office?

Our Times: Black, White, and Red All Over at a New Orleans Newspaper

James Karst, senior editor at the *Times-Picayune*, continued the story:

> "Are you Mr. Osmond?" demanded Houston.
>
> "Yes," responded Osmond.
>
> Houston promptly rapped the editor in the head with his walking stick, and a scuffle ensued. Drawn by the commotion, one of Osmond's employees, Adolph Zennecke, ran up to the desk.
>
> Brewster then drew a gun. So did Houston. Osmond reached into his desk and pulled out his own gun. Who fired first is unclear, but all three pulled the trigger, and bullets whizzed through the room.
>
> Seconds later, startled passers-by on Camp Street witnessed Houston tearing out of the office, bleeding from the right hand. He paused in the middle of the street and looked momentarily up at the office where the shootout had taken place then crossed the street to a store, where he sought treatment.
>
> Brewster came out next, but not nearly as fast. He had been shot four times, including once in the chest. He struggled as he made his way to a nearby bank and upon entering, collapsed into a chair. Bloody footprints marked his path all the way back to the newspaper office, where bullets had torn through walls, lodged in desks, and even pierced a picture of the newly opened World's Industrial and Cotton Centennial Exposition hanging on the wall. ["The shots seemed to have been aimed without much precision," noted the *Picayune*.]
>
> Osmond was the next to dash out the door, blowing a whistle to summon the police. He had been hit in the arm and was in considerable pain.
>
> All three were taken to Charity Hospital. Houston and Osmond were not badly injured and soon were released. But Brewster didn't make it. He died the next morning.
>
> Houston, the tax collector and brother of the judge, was booked with shooting with intent to kill and was released on

bond. Osmond and Zennecke were held without bail, the former on a murder charge and the latter as an accessory.

"What was the cause of the difficulty?" a reporter for the *Daily Picayune* asked Osmond in a jailhouse interview.

"I can't exactly say, although I have my suspicions," Osmond replied.

"It is said that it was on account of an article about Judge Houston published last week," the reporter pressed.

"That may be," Osmond conceded.

Brewster's deep political connections are clear from the long list of dignitaries at his funeral. Pallbearers included a city council member, a judge, a US senator, and the police commissioner. Mayor J. Valsin Guillotte, the parish coroner, several other judges, and the state attorney general were among those who took part in the funeral procession to St. Patrick's Cemetery No. 2.

Tried for assault and attempted murder, James Houston was acquitted. Call it justice New Orleans style 1885. A grand jury declined to indict Osmond and Zennecke, although their escape from death was just a short reprieve. In 1887, Zennecke was shot and killed at the *Mascot* office, while Osmond, after being deputized by the Plaquemines Parish sheriff, was killed that same year by a fugitive from justice.

According to an editorial about the 1885 shootout at the *Mascot* office published in the *St. Landry Democrat*, "Osmond may be a very bad man, through the columns of The Mascot; but in this particular case he should not be blamed if he had killed both Houston and Brewster—he was fighting in self-defense."

The Wallace women claimed they were unaware that James Houston had attacked the *Mascot* staff in defense of Dora's honor (or at least partly so, as he was also defending his family name, and besides, we think James just liked a good fight—he certainly got into plenty of them).

"They did not see the article, the daily papers did not reprint it and the Wallaces say they did not know and Houston did not tell them that Dora had also figured in the paper," ran an article in the Friday, October 30, 1885, edition of the *(Shreveport, LA)*

Times. "Being in such ignorance, they sat with open window and looked at Brewster's funeral possession as it passed their house, not guessing why so many people looked at them with curious interest. Had they an inkling of the truth they would not have been so conspicuous on the occasion."

But really, one has to wonder, how had they not heard? And didn't they love attention? We think they sat there knowing full well what had happened, enjoyed the attention, and knew it was good advertising for their charms.

As for J. D. Houston, his brutish temper continued on. Three years later, he would be involved in the assassination of Patrick Mealey, the New Orleans police commissioner. The gun used in the shooting was bought by a man who handed the shopkeeper a note written by Houston instructing him to sell it to him.

Probably James's greatest contribution to violence, mayhem, and general despicable behavior was his leading role in what was called the "largest mass lynching in America," which occurred on March 14, 1891, after the acquittal of several Italians who had been charged with the murder of Police Chief Patrick Hennessey. (Being high up in police administration was obviously as dangerous as working for the *Mascot*.) Hennessey, who was shot while walking home from work, lived long enough to chase after his assailant, returning fire, before collapsing to the ground. When asked who'd shot him, he seemed to say "the dagoes," using a derogatory term for Italians, who at that time in the United States were very much discriminated against.

His dying accusation resulted in the arrest of nineteen Italian men, most of whom were Sicilian immigrants. (The common thinking back then seemed to be the only thing worse than Italians were southern Italians.) At the conclusion of the trial, a jury acquitted many of them; others weren't tried because of lack of evidence. But they remained in jail while other charges were cooked up.

As far as Houston was concerned, that didn't constitute justice as he saw it. Rabble-rousing with three other men, they managed to rile up a crowd of thousands. Their furor was also incited by several newspapers of the day (though the *Picayune* wisely cautioned against retribution), including the *Daily States*, which ran the following: "Rise, people of New Orleans! Alien hands of oath-bound assassins have set the blot of a martyr's blood upon your vaunted civilization! Your laws, in the very Temple of Justice, have been bought off, and suborders have caused to be turned loose upon your streets the midnight murderers of David C. Hennessy, in whose premature grave the very majesty of our American law lies buried with his mangled corpse—the corpse of him who in life was the representative, the conservator of your peace and dignity."

As the mob was breaking down the jail doors with a battering ram, prison warden Lemuel Davis opened the cells of the nineteen prisoners, urging them to hide. Eight managed to do so, but the other eleven were either dragged outside and hanged or shot or beaten to death inside the jail.

It was the work of the devil, and that best describes James Houston, who in less than three years would die of leukemia on January 29, 1894.

Husband versus Judge

History has not left us many clues about Edward Findlay. Searching under New Orleans artists doesn't yield much information about his art, so we're left to assume that he wasn't very successful. Was he also clueless about the relationship between his lovely young wife and Judge Houston? News accounts say that Findlay was extremely upset with the *Mascot*'s story, asking Judge Houston what he intended to do about it. That perhaps offers insight into Edward's personality. Instead of taking matters in his own hands, which seemed to be the New Orleans way, he wanted Houston to deal with it.

For his part, Houston, perhaps knowing more about Dora's honor (or lack of it) than Findlay, said he would sue. Findlay wanted to join the suit, and when he discovered Houston had never gotten around to filing it, he confronted him. Houston told Findlay that he was waiting for his brother to return from

Europe; however, even after James returned, he still didn't file. Finally poor, clueless Edward realized he had no plans to do so.

Findlay confronted Houston again at 222 Canal Street, and before long, they were shouting at each other. Dora got involved as well, though whether she took sides or was just trying to calm them down wasn't reported. The fight ended with Houston angrily leaving the house.

The two men didn't speak again until both showed up in Emporia to save Minnie.

Dora had a theory about the *Mascot*'s article—one that made her quite the innocent. It seems that she and Minnie had gone with the judge to the Rex Ball but left early. Maybe Judge Houston had later been seen at the masquerade ball with a woman with a figure similar to hers, Dora wondered. We wonder if Edward bought her version of events. We can tell you that we don't.

But that was Dora's story, and she was sticking to it, though she also had another backup explanation. She told a reporter she and her husband and their family had been living in Texas for the last two years, and so she couldn't have attended the Rex Ball, as she wasn't even in New Orleans.

The prestigious Rex Ball marks the end of Mardi Gras and is an extravaganza of music, pageantry, stunning costumes, dancing, marches, and parades. Even the invitations for the 1885 season were works of art. The ball is one of the prominent events for the Mardi Gras season, so it's intriguing that Houston would show up there with a married woman and her sister who had just turned sixteen. All this was, of course, an irresistible target for the *Mascot*.

In the mix of all this was Walkup, who was in town about that time and claimed he had stopped at the *Mascot* office to talk about the article. No one was there, he said.

Wallace was becoming even more concerned about his daughter's life at 222 Canal Street and wrote a long letter of advice urging her to become emancipated. She could then stay with his relatives in Wyoming County, New York, and complete her education. The letter was intercepted by Elizabeth, who answered the door and refused to deliver it to Minnie. Even if the letter had reached Minnie, do we really believe she would have moved to Upstate New York and gone back to school? It's very doubtful. Minnie and her mother were very close, and they had other plans. Minnie's looks were her fortune; why should they be wasted in a classroom?

When the city learned Houston was in Emporia, the *Mascot* staff just could not—and we mean *could not*—resist writing an unflattering article about his trip. It was also surmised that Houston's affections seemed to have switched from Dora to Minnie.

A Father's Tale

Whether he was drunk, delusional, or just mean, James Wallace, obviously working on earning the title of worst dad in the world, told *Mascot* reporters that he doubted whether Minnie was really his daughter. He also questioned the legality of her marriage to Walkup. Even if true, it certainly wasn't going to help Minnie out of her current predicament.

Later, either sobering up or realizing he might be killing the golden goose in terms of the Walkup money Minnie stood to inherit if she didn't hang, Wallace backtracked, saying he was never aware of any lewdness on the part of his former wife and never doubted Minnie was his child. He had in fact made these accusations before, and maybe they were true, but why bring them up now with Minnie's life hanging in the balance?

By then, his accusations and the *Mascot* article had made their way to Emporia and gave the townspeople there another reason to question Minnie's character.

James Wallace attempted to change the narrative. He ordered a copy of James and Minnie's marriage certificate from Covington, Kentucky, and within ten minutes he had forwarded it on to Emporia. Though he said he hadn't been allowed to see Minnie much since the divorce, he wrote fondly of her to many, including Mrs. Augustus Wilson, a wealthy Kansas widow who had been the "lady commissioner to the last exposition," meaning the World's Industrial and Cotton Centennial Exposition—the same event that had brought Walkup to New Orleans and the boardinghouse where he met Minnie and ultimately led to his death.

For some unexplained reason, Mrs. Wilson had incurred the wrath of Julia Ward Howe, the founder of the Girl Scouts and a New Orleans resident. But that is a historical aside. Mrs. Wilson, perhaps seeing the strong father-daughter bond, took up Minnie's cause and sent her own lawyer, E. C. Ward of Parsons, Kansas, to assist the defense.

Wallace was planning to come to Kansas to assist his daughter in her time of need. But Minnie—and her attorney—didn't want him anywhere near Emporia. In a move that proves the brains in the family came from the maternal side, she wrote an amazingly well-crafted letter (she must have learned something during her convent school days) that showed her worthy of Machiavelli. Her missive, an amazing example of the well-bred training that Elizabeth Wallace had instilled in her daughters along with their beguiling ways, was crafted to flatter her father while ensuring he stayed far away. No matter what her crimes (and she would have plenty more to come), Minnie knew how to handle herself in a crisis.

> My Dear Father.
> I have just finished reading the letter you wrote Lawyer Scott. You cannot imagine how great my joy was and how I felt of my father. Can you wonder at Mr. Jay's indignation when he heard that it was you who gave the Mascot all of its information and that you were helping to convict your own child?
> Think of it and you will see that you or I or any other person would feel the same to a man who could be low enough to do anything like that. A great injustice has been done you and I ask your pardon for having entertained unkind thoughts of you. Oh father, I am happier today than I have been for a very long time, for I am sure that you now love me and always have. I know that you want me to come before the world pure and vindicated. I hope the time is near when I can put my arms around your neck and say father you have helped me.

Mr. Scott told me to mention to you for him that he advised you not to come to Emporia. I will explain why when I see you. I hope soon to have that pleasure. Write soon.

Believe me your loving daughter. Minnie.

Think about this letter. Reread it even. What we have is a girl who is sixteen years old, accused of murder with serious evidence indicating she had poisoned her husband, facing the hangman's noose. Her father had betrayed her by recounting the family scandals, and then he wants to come north to "help" defend her, loose cannon that he is. It's a situation that calls for a seasoned diplomat.

Minnie's letter is a masterpiece of art and tact and totally hysterics-free. There's no wailing, no anger, no accusations. She handles him brilliantly, flatters him, and, at the same time, asks him not to come to Emporia. And all from a teenager under extreme stress. How many adults could have handled this as well as our Minnie?

No wonder she would go on to get away with murder more than once.

As for the home at 222 Canal Street and the family who lived there, the *Topeka Daily Capital* opined, considering the cast of characters:

> Richer and racier developments may be expected if poisoning is proved to have been the cause of death; but it must be remembered that fertile brains are working, and busy hands are ready and willing, and after all it maybe a case of sensation spoiled. Be that as it may, however, we have published sufficient facts—incontrovertible facts—of the character and the standing of the Wallace family to prove them adventurers or adventuresses of a bold, undaunted type.
>
> As to their breeding and accomplishments, we have it from her husband that Mrs. Wallace, mother of Minnie, can scarcely write.

That final parting shot may be true. A look at the wedding license for James R. Wallace and Elizabeth Egan Kirby on July 12, 1865, shows the groom's very clear and concise signature while Elizabeth's first signature is crossed out because it appears that she misspelled her last name. She re-signs it below, but again the spelling is very labored. What should be a *K* is written over with another misshapen letter; the *i* isn't completed, and the small *r* is backward. Elizabeth, indeed, didn't even know how to sign her name. But she knew how to teach her daughter to marry for money and get away with murder.

3

DON'T CRY FOR ME, EMPORIA

Great Balls of Fire!

Cinderella's stepmother, as evil as she was, was an amateur compared to Minnie, who after landing James Walkup, dropped all pretense of affection for his daughters. What was the difference between these two stepmothers? Well, let's start on August 18, when Libbie Walkup returned from Colorado to find several of her cloaks were missing.

Minnie, of course, denied knowing where they were. Libbie wasn't buying that and retorted that maybe they'd been in one of the boxes Minnie had shipped to New Orleans. Turns out Libbie was half right. Mary Moss, the live-in maid who may or may not have been James's mistress (it was that kind of home), discovered some of Libbie's clothes hidden in Minnie's closet.

Stolen clothes soon turned out to be the least of Libbie's problems. Around nine o'clock one night, Libbie turned off the gaslight in her second-floor room, placed two teaspoons of yellow "Persian Insect Powder" that she'd purchased to keep away mosquitos in a dust pan, lit it with a match and climbed into bed. As it was a hot summer's night, the door to her father and stepmother's room across the hall was open. Willie was asleep on the porch, and Mary Moss was sleeping elsewhere in the house.

"It was almost an hour after I went to bed before I fell asleep," Libbie would later testify, noting her bed was about eight to nine feet from the doorway—a pertinent fact in trying to establish how the fire might have occurred. "I was awakened about 11 or 12; I could not say which. I awakened and felt that my feet were too warm. I looked and saw a blaze at my feet and one at my shoulder. The bedding (a sheet and two quilts) was on fire. The blaze at my feet was, I think, five inches high, while that at my head was hardly so large, and was just commencing to burn."

Running into her father's room, she grabbed the washbowl and used the water in it to douse the flames. Neither Minnie nor James stirred, and Libbie, concerned about her father's health, said she decided not to wake them and instead, looking to see what could have caused the fire, discovered a burned-out match at the foot of her bed. As she talked, the prosecution displayed the two-and-a-half-foot-long burn at the foot of the quilt and the smaller burned spot on the sheet.

Minnie, for her part, knew nothing about the fire. Absolutely nothing. Honest.

"I went to the porch because it was cool out there and it was warm on the inside," she said at the coroner's inquest. "I do not remember about Miss Walkup's bed being afire. She told Mr. Walker's mother and showed her the quilt. That was the first I knew of it; I do not know when it occurred. Mrs. Walkup did not say how it occurred. Miss Walkup said there was a match on the bed; she said the match caught after some time in the night, she did not know how."

After Walkup's death, the police searched the house and found an empty bottle of strychnine in a desk in Libbie's room. Libbie denied ever buying poison and claimed not to know how it got in her room, pointing out the door to the room was seldom locked even when she wasn't home.

Minnie, perhaps trying to throw more suspicions on Libbie, said she'd purchased a bottle of strychnine at Bates Drugstore and carried it home in her hand satchel, which she'd hung up in the hallway. Later, she found the bottle was gone. She asked Mary Moss if she'd seen it. Moss said no. The next day, saying she needed arsenic this time (Minnie seemed to alternate in the types of poisons she purchased) to mix with urine to take out a stain, Minnie sent Moss to buy another bottle. Her story worked on two levels, providing a reason to buy more and implying that Libbie had stolen the bottle and used its contents to poison her father.

Besides being used to kill vermin (and unwanted husbands), in Minnie's day poisons like arsenic and strychnine were ingredients in cleaning and beauty preparations. Brands like the popular Dr. Rose's French Arsenic Complexion Wafers were available at drugstores and even at Sears. Applied externally or chewed in wafer form, the arsenic constricted the capillaries, whitening the skin—a look considered beautiful and also indicative of social status. A well-to-do woman didn't have to labor outside like a farmer's wife. She could instead spend her days inside, waited on by servants.

Arsenic had other purposes, too. Arsenic eaters, despite all the medical knowledge available even back in the early 1800s, believed that steadily consuming an increasing amount of the poison helped increase sexual vigor (the nineteenth-century equivalent to today's Viagra), assisted breathing, and made the user stronger and more courageous. It also was a treatment for venereal disease.

"I think it very likely that he took the arsenic with the idea that it would excite vital forces that had been made dormant by dissipation," Dr. S. G. Colburn said when asked by a reporter for the *Kansas City Journal* what the effect of arsenic would be. "In fact, I know from an Emporia newsman who was here recently that just before he died he purchased some stuff at a drug store and gave a reason which any of the medical fraternity would easily understand, especially if they were acquainted with Mr. Walkup. While arsenic would not be the best article for producing the effect that Mr. Walkup desired, I think it more than probable that he took it with the idea it was just what he needed."

Dr. Joshua Thorne told the same reporter that arsenic is an accumulative poison and may be taken in minute qualities for a long time without producing serious consequences until suddenly the most disastrous results will occur.

"Do you think it likely that Mr. Walker poisoned himself?" asked the reporter.

"I think it's very likely, more so than his young wife poisoned him" was the response.

Another doctor weighed in.

Dr. J. W. Trueworthy, who lived in Emporia two years before the murder, said he had been Mr. Walkup's physician.

"I know at the time he took Fowler's Solution in large quantities," he said, about a name brand potassium arsenic solution prescribed as a general tonic from about 1786 to 1936 in both the United States and England.

The defense also brought up Eben Baldwin's testimony to the grand jury that on their trip to New Orleans, Walkup, who had visited a pharmacy, had developed violent cramps, pain, and vomiting, the same symptoms he exhibited shortly before dying. Could he have been nibbling arsenic to get ready for the ladies in New Orleans?

The prosecution was ready for this argument. Sure, Walkup had bought medicine on the journey south. But no, it wasn't arsenic.

With testimony like this, it's no wonder that people waited at train stations throughout the Midwest for the latest editions of the *Kansas City Journal* and the *Times-Picayune* to arrive. In Emporia's largest courtroom was reconfigured to accommodate three hundred people but there still were long lines of people waiting to get it. Those lucky enough to get a seat, knew better than to vacate it for any reason. Some filled their pockets with gingerbread and apples to nibble on throughout the day. Like many trials of that era, the majority (about two-thirds) of those attending the trial were women—a fact that never failed to upset newspaper editors who wrote scathing editorials about how they should instead be home taking care of their children and preparing dinner for their husbands.

What Minnie wore was also part of the fascination, and male reporters began to write like fashionistas. On October 22, 1885, the *Times-Picayune* reported, "Minnie was dressed as usual in a close-fitting black cashmere jersey and the skirt trimmed with chenille fringe, with white ruching around her neck and in the sleeves. She did not wear a bonnet."

It was noted Mrs. Wallace, sitting next to her daughter, also looked stylish in her elegant black silk dress with white collar and cuffs. She wore brown kid gloves and carried a ladies' hand satchel.

Stockpiling Poison

It turned out that though she had only been in Emporia for two weeks before James died, Minnie had found the time to visit most of the druggists in town.

She'd bought eight grams of poison from Moses Bates—only one-half gram is needed to kill someone. Bates asked her to sign the poison book while he went to wrap it up. After she left, he noticed she had left the purpose section empty.

Druggist R. B. Kelly said that about the twelfth or thirteenth of August, she'd handed him a small white powder, saying it had been given to her by a lady friend in New Orleans and asked him what it was. Either quinine, strychnine, or morphine, he told her, but as they resembled each other so closely, it was impossible to tell without careful testing. Minnie returned on August 16 to purchase arsenic. Four days later, said Benjamin Weldon, another druggist in town, he sold her arsenic as well.

Dr. J. A. Moore, describing himself as somewhat acquainted with the defendant, testified that around August 15, he had examined two grams of a white bulk powder she brought to his store and told her it was quinine. Moore's clerk Frank McCullough was there when the conversation took place.

On August 14, Minnie walked into the drugstore belonging to W. R. Irwin and requested ten cents' worth of strychnine. As he was measuring it out, she changed her mind and asked for fifteen cents' worth instead. When Irwin handed her the poison record and asked her to sign it, she handed it back to him, saying, "You don't think I am going to commit suicide, do you?" When he asked why she wanted it, Minnie said she needed it in a preparation she was making but refused to tell him anything more. Irwin refused to sell it to her, a conversation overheard by Joseph Murphy, who had a stationery store inside the drugstore.

Despite the testimony of the two men, Minnie denied it had happened.

She'd also stopped at Charles Ryder's. He wanted her to sign the poison book.

"Why do I have to do that?" she asked.

"Because it's the law" was the reply.

The white powder that Minnie wanted tested had been purchased in Cincinnati, Ohio, just across the river from Covington, where she and James had married. Had she decided to murder Walkup before they went on their honeymoon? We don't know. What we do know is that Minnie had flawless skin, so it would seem she had little need of arsenic.

Fortunately for Minnie, her guardian, William Jay, found the perfect witness to rebut this testimony—a Kansas City doctor, Charles W. Scott, who attested to Walkup's need to "keep up" with his teenage wife. According to Scott, in the fall of 1884, Walkup had stopped by his office, complaining of abdominal pains. He told Scott he taking was a combination of arsenic and opium prescribed for treating a chronic disease (he was also taking mercury) as well as using arsenic as a sexual stimulant. All this was news to the physicians who were treating Walkup in Emporia, including Dr. Jacobs, his doctor in his final days.

Dr. Scott's testimony was a bombshell indicating, as it did, that Walkup had accidentally poisoned himself. But if Walkup was buying arsenic, he certainly wasn't doing so in Emporia, as his signature wasn't found in any of the druggists' poison books. Sure, he traveled a lot in his business, but wouldn't he have bought it locally as well? Also, though Scott testified that Walkup was taking mercury, which was a common—and itself a rather deadly—treatment for syphilis, an autopsy showed no sign of the disease. But then again, forensic medicine back then certainly wasn't cutting edge, and Walkup certainly frequented the types of places where a man could easily pick up a host of bad things.

Another damning fact—not only had Minnie bought enough poison to murder half the town, she also insisted on being the only one to administer Walkup's medications in those final days. The prosecution made much of that, alleging she had substituted poison for the potions prescribed by his doctors.

Minnie's memory problems led her to deny trying to purchase poison.

Then there was her kindly and caring trip to get James the soda pop he desired after he ate some canned oysters. He'd been feeling better, but after drinking the soda Minnie had purchased for him, he became very ill again. Could it have something to do with the other stop she made on her way home—the one where she purchased twenty-five cents of arsenic?

Mr. Jay's High Hopes

Minnie had perfectly captivated William Jay, who told a newsman for the *Times-Picayune* that if Minnie was acquitted, she would be coming to stay at his house, possibly to remain there for the winter. It's easy to believe Minnie was promising just that, as Jay was spending big time to keep Minnie from the gallows, including paying the fees and expenses of a well-respected attorney named Dodd from Hazlehurst.

Jay, who so fervently believed in her innocence, finally took the step that, besides her own testimony, most likely tilted the balance in her favor. A man most esteemed, he took the stand with a story of his own to tell.

Would you believe—and the prosecution certainly didn't—that in July before the marriage, Jay had run in to Walkup on the streets of Emporia, and the two went to Jay's office to conduct some business? When they were done, Walkup complained of not feeling well and asked Jay for water and a knife. Jay didn't observe what happened next, but a few minutes later, he saw white powder on the knife and watched as Walkup put the powder in a glass of water that he then drank. Handing the knife back to Jay, Walkup cautioned him to make sure the blade was clean.

Jay wanted to know why.

Arsenic was Walkup's succinct answer.

Prosecutors found the timing of Jay's story, including the fact that he'd never mentioned this very important encounter before, puzzling. He hadn't, he said, because Minnie's attorney had asked him not to. That also was incomprehensible. His story was tantamount to giving Minnie a get-out-of-jail-free card. Why wait to use it?

When the prosecutor asked Jay if his story had just suddenly popped into his mind, Jay asked rather snarkily if he would be so kind as to define the word *popped*.

The prosecutor just as tartly replied, "Don't you understand English?"

Though considered a very honest man, Jay had told people that nothing would prevent him from doing what he thought was right. It would seem that his deeply held belief in Minnie's innocence led him to perjure himself—for the greater good and all that.

Someone would remark, some twelve years later, when Minnie's second husband, John Ketcham, died in suspicious circumstances, that it was lucky Jay wasn't alive, as this would surely have killed him.

Blaming the Victim

One thing is very certain that if Mr. Walkup was as corrupt and rotten as the defense makes him out he ought to have died long ago.

—*Topeka Daily Capital*, Friday, October 30, 1885

The defense also offered another theory—if Walkup didn't accidently kill himself from an overdose, maybe he finally had succeeded in committing suicide:

Evidence was adduced at the trial of Minnie Wallace Walkup, charged with having poisoned her husband, that on the day before his death, Mr. Walkup tried to commit suicide by shooting himself with a revolver.

Mr. Walkup told a neighbor that the shooting was accidental, but Mrs. Walkup said that he had attempted suicide because of despondency caused by the receipt of a letter from his daughter severely criticizing him for having married Mrs. Walkup.

—*New York Times*, October 23, 1885

On the day of the shooting, Walkup told I. Severy that the revolver went off accidentally and nearly shot him in the head. Witnesses described the hole in the wall made by the shot, and during cross-examination, the defense pointed out the angle of the hole could have been made either by Walkup standing up or sitting down to shoot himself in the head. It could not have happened by an accidental discharge if he were either standing or sitting.

The Verdict

The jury's decision didn't come easy. On the first ballot they'd been split—six voting to convict and six to acquit. The next day, three more jurors switched to innocent, but the other three still held firm. A third ballot remained nine to three. Then one of the remaining three changed his vote to not guilty, making it ten to two. Minnie was moving further from the hangman's noose.

Finally the other two gave in. Minnie would go free. It had taken fifty-six hours.

Receiving notice that deliberations were finished, Judge Gray ordered court to reconvene. Dressed in a close-fitting blue tricot dress, white lace collar and cuffs, Minnie did not exhibit any undue nervousness or expectancy when she took her seat along with Mr. Jay and her attorney, though spectators noted she looked very pale.

It wasn't from fear, as she'd already been told the verdict.

After the foreman stood to deliver the verdict—"We, the jury, find the defendant not guilty"—the cheering in the courtroom was deafening. Minnie crossed over to the jury box to thank them. Then she shook hands with Judge Gray. Mrs. Wallace, who had just entered the courtroom, hurried over to her daughter, embracing her, and the two began crying. Turning to Jay, Elizabeth threw her arms around him and gave him a kiss. Next, she too thanked the jurors. Never one to underplay the drama, she next turned to the judge and, falling on her knees, cried, "God bless you, Judge! God bless you. You have saved my child."

Those Wallace women knew how to stage a scene.

County Attorney Feighan, who remained in the courtroom after the verdict, turned to a juror and said that though he didn't admire the verdict, they had been a good jury and he was fully satisfied with it.

One juror told a reporter from the *Emporia Daily News* that he voted to acquit despite his doubts. Why? Because he didn't want to see Minnie hang. When the reporter pointed out that nobody had been executed for quite a while in Kansas, the juror said he knew that.

"But there might come along a governor who might take it into head to hang every one of the prisoners in the penitentiary who have been found guilty of murder in the first degree, and I don't think there was anyone on the jury who wanted that for Mrs. Walkup."

There obviously wouldn't be any justice for the doomed bridegroom.

Celebration

Outside the courthouse, Minnie, Mr. Jay, and Mr. Scott were surrounded by a cheering crowd, and the telegraph station was kept busy with the hundreds of congratulatory telegrams arriving from around the country.

Jay had planned a "blowout" celebration, with a brass band, and the jurors were invited. Minnie gave kisses to more than a few.

After her second husband's death, Minnie would look back at the trial and in her typical way, ignore that it took the jury fifty-six hours to reach a not guilty verdict.

> I was tried and acquitted by 12 men who listened as attentively to the prosecution as to the defense. We've proved to the entire satisfaction of those 12 men by the testimony of leading professionals from Kansas City and Topeka that Mr. Walkup had for years been addicted to use of arsenic. We proved that he sent to Kansas City to a certain druggist for years for it; and that he seldom bought arsenic in Emporia because he feared the use of it would be discovered by his friends. I was put on the stand to testify. The court room was crowded. People were eager to hear what I have to say. I was on the stand perhaps an hour—it of course seemed an eternity to me—and in all the vast crowd they were the two faces that appeared to me. One was the face of my good friend, Mr. Jay, and the other the white, delicate face of my beloved mother. When I left the stand the judge and the jury were weeping. The young lady stenographer was so hysterical that she could not write. Someone after said that I was the only person in the courtroom who was not weeping.

Minnie was a historic revisionist, rewriting her autobiography as she lived it.

Cold as Ice

Fifteen years old and just out of the convent school when she met her first husband and halfway to her seventeenth birthday when he died, who was Minnie Wallace beyond the gorgeous face and form?

Whether she was born bad we don't know. But her looks were such that she certainly was well on the road to acclaim when she won a beautiful baby contest while still an infant. We know she attended two convent schools and lived in a cramped but popular boardinghouse owned by her mother, who counted several high-powered gentlemen among the family's friends.

Walkup wasn't her first victim, though he was the first to die. According to Sally Asher, before Minnie met James, there had been some trouble with a clerk who, so taken by her "dark Creole beauty," had stolen money to buy her jewelry.

We also know she was impossibly cool under pressure. Reporters raved about her looks and her calmness in the face of adversity. There is no reason to doubt either observation.

Usually, the press portrayed Minnie in a fairly positive, if not glowing, light. Sure, there were some snide and sarcastic references, but few, if any, really analyzed Minnie's personality. One exception is the following article, which first ran in the *Kansas City Times* and was picked up by the local Emporia newspaper shortly after Minnie's acquittal. The reporter seems to have gotten it right—not even knowing the other deaths and deceptions that were in the future.

Her Face Her Fortune

Some of the Strange Characteristics of the Defendant in the Late Walkup Poisoning Case

The Cold-Blooded Manner in Which the Widow Treated Matters Terrifying to Ordinary Humanity.

The Beauty's Inordinate Vanity Displayed at All Times and Under All Circumstances

Street Parade on Which the Young Widow Receives Attentions from Numerous Admirers

Arranging for a Big Reception—Sitting for a New Photograph—The Fanatical Guardian's Doings.

Emporia Daily News, Tuesday November 10, 1885

It will be a long time before the people of this ordinarily quiet village are done talking about the Walker case. By the verdict of twelve farmers Mrs. Wallace is a free woman, but by that same verdict of "not guilty" she is not by any means a spotless creature.

When riding the streets Mrs. Walkup beamed generously and kept her eyes open to see known friends and enemies. She was dressed in her blue surge, with scarlet trimmings and wore a white veil over a small round hat. Miss Jay (Mr. Jay's unmarried daughter who had attended the trial religiously) stopped at numerous stores along Commercial Street, the widow remaining in the carriage and during these times she was often visited by the ladies and other friends and chatted with her on various topics. She called on several persons who had befriended her and it was late in the evening before she concluded her sightseeing and her visiting and return to the home of Mr. Jay where she is now domiciled.

The air with which she gazed at persons whom she met was in keeping with her demeanor everywhere. She tried to out-stare those who look curiously at her, and if anybody expected to see her cast down by the fearful ordeal through which she had passed, he was badly mistaken.

A great deal has been said about her nerve but to anyone who has studied her character, another name would suggest itself. An instance or two will suffice to illustrate the true nature of this quality. Walkup's autopsy was held in their sleeping room upstairs.

The Beauty's Heartlessness

The doctors cut him to pieces, removing his liver, heart, stomach, in fact removing nearly everything else. The bed was in a frightful condition, the remains were scattered about the room in vessels, and the air was horrible, and yet within an hour after the body had been taken downstairs, the widow went to the room, still uncleaned, locked herself in and proceeded to undress herself as calmly as if there was no ghastly evidence of death within a hundred miles of her.

Then when the neighbors offered to sit up with her tonight as her husband's dead body was in the house, she declared it made no difference to her as she would just as soon stay in the house alone as have anyone with her. People who knew these facts were not surprised that she could outface a cross examination whose questions would have been like knife thrusts to a sensitive nature.

The late defendant has been having a kind of a picnic ever since her discharge from the custody of her friends, the Sheriff. She appeared on the streets yesterday in company with Mr. Jay in the forenoon and in the buggy with Miss Jay in the afternoon. In the morning she went to the court house where she gathered up the few things she had left there and she then took a quiet farewell of her old quarters.

Then she went to two photographers, where she sat for her pictures, securing a good negative in three or four different positions. It is understood that she is to get a commission on the sale of these pictures. She has had no photographs taken since her marriage, and although she has not changed his appearance very materially since the time she met J. R Walkup, yet her old pictures do not do the justice which she desires.

When the young bride came from New Orleans she complained that northern people were far more sparing in their appraisal of her beauty than those with whom she been accustomed to live. When Walkup was dead, and people flocked to her house by the hundreds she sat with folded arms and exhibited her charms unmindful of the remarks made by strangers, and not kindly ones, either.

Movements of the Fanatical Friend

Mr. Jay yesterday attempted to secure the keys to the house in which the widow lived with Walkup and in which he died. It has remained closed ever since Mrs. Walkup was taken to jail, and the administrator of the estate, Major Hood, has the keys. He is temporarily out of the city, and no one felt authorized to give up the key in his absence. Some speculation was indulged as to whether Mrs. Walkup intended to take possession of the homestead, but in view of her declaration that she does not want any of Walkup's property, it is not believed she will attempt to hold the house. It is intimated that the administrator will be in no haste to give up anything, even should she change her mind.

When the trial was on, she eyed the interested crowd with complacency, and received her numerous callers with a welcome, and every mention of her in the newspapers was perused with unfeigned pleasure.

After it was all over and a score or more were congratulating her at the informal reception held at Jay's the night of the acquittal, she said to newspaperman who remarked that he was probably making his last professional call on her, "Oh, I hope the newspapers are not going to drop me as soon is all that."

Not to worry. Minnie would be a meal ticket for reporters for decades to come.

4

PARDON MY DUST

Nonstop to Nowhere

RETURNING HOME TO 222 CANAL STREET AFTER HER acquittal and celebratory party, where she kissed a couple of the older men on the jury (at their request), Minnie again became the focus of an adoring group of older male admirers who flocked to Mrs. Wallace's boardinghouse.

One such admirer was the sixty-year-old (even older than Walkup) former US senator and Louisiana governor William Pitt Kellogg, who through various complicated and corrupt schemes had amassed a fortune. Minnie would turn seventeen in January 1886. Soon the two would embark on a cross-country tour by train that was reported with wonder and disgust in US newspapers. That's a story in itself, and we'll get to it soon. First, though, let's go back to Emporia, where Minnie was gone but not forgotten and a new scandal was brewing. But first a little background.

Before leaving Emporia, Minnie had insinuated to several reporters that she might be carrying Walkup's child, most likely as a ploy to garner a larger share of his insurance policy. That was peanuts compared to what happened while James Walkup's will was being probated.

Walkup

Some Remarkable Deceptions by Sheriff
Wilhite's Son and by the Janitor.
The Legitimacy of an Expected Heir to the
Walker Estate Brought in Question.
Emporia Weekly News, Thursday, December 24, 1885

The question arising as to the possibility of a co-heir in the person of a child which is yet to arrive by J. R. Walkup by his third wife, Minnie Wallace Walkup, doubts in regard to the legitimacy of that child were expressed, owing to certain facts and circumstances connected with the sojourn of Mrs. Walker and the county jail in the city.

Accordingly, the different attorneys connected with the case secure the depositions of Oscar Wilhite, the 19-year-old son of Sheriff Wilhite, and Edward Gutekunst, the janitor of the courthouse, a boy about the same age as young Wilhite, to the effect that each of these boys have, on two different occasions during her confinement in the county jail last September and October, occupied the same bed with Mrs. Walker, at her request.

These depositions were taken in the office of Kellogg and Sedgwick and have been read by a news reporter. It will probably be filed with the clerk of the District Court next Monday and the course of time will tell whether or not they will accomplish the purpose desired.

Depositions

They More Than Sustain the Allegations
Emporia Weekly News, December 20, 1885

Q: You may state your name, age and residence.

A: Oscar Wilhite; Emporia, Kansas; 19 the tenth of last November.

Q: How long have you lived in Emporia?

A: About 10 years.

Q: You may state what relation you are to sheriff J.H. Wilhite of this county.

A: I am his son.

Q: Are you acquainted with the defendants, Wm. B. Walkup, Martha Hood and Lizzie Walkup or either of them?

A. I am acquainted with Lizzie Walkup and I know Mrs. Hood by sight and I don't know Mr. Walkup at all.

Q. Are you acquainted with Minnie Wallace Walkup?

A. Yes, sir.

Q. How long have been acquainted with her?

A. Since she came to the court house about September 1, 1885.

Q. You may state how your acquaintance with her continued?

A. Till after the trial.

Q. What do you mean?

A. Her trial.

Q. For what?

A. For murdering J. H. Walkup.

Q: You may state whether or not you were living at home with your father at the court house during this time.

A: Yes, sir.

Q. State whether or not you had sex and intercourse with her at either of this time?

A. Yes sir, both.

Q. At whose invitation was it that you had sexual intercourse with Minnie Wallace Walkup these two times.

A. It was at her own.

Q. When was the first of these occasions when you had sexual intercourse with her?

A. It was on a Saturday night about the 3rd of October.

Q. When was the last time?

A. It was on Sunday night—the next night.

Q. Do you know of any other man besides yourself being alone with Minnie Wallace Walkup in her room at night?

A. None except Edward Gutekunst.

Deposition of Edward Gutekunst

Q. You may state whether or not you were ever in the room alone with her (Minnie Walkup) in her room alone during the night time or any portion of it.

A. Yes, sir. I believe I was.

Q. Was it before or after she had gone to bed for the night?

A. Both before and after.

Q. At whose invitation or suggestion was it that you went into her room after she had gone to bed?

A. At her own.

Q. You may now state what you and she did while alone with her in her room at that time.

A. I was in there several times; talked to her; took a dress to her from another room and laid it on a chair or bed.

Q. State whether or not she more than once invited you into her room, either after she had gone to bed or when wholly or partially undressed.

A. Yes, sir.

Q. You may state whether or not during your acquaintance with Minnie Wallace Walkup at the court house, you ever had sexual intercourse with her.

A. Yes, I believe I did.

Q. More than once?

A. A couple of times.

Q. At whose invitation or suggestion was it that you had sexual intercourse with her?

A. It was her invitation and at Oscar Wilhite's suggestion.

Q. You may state whether or not you know of any other man visiting her alone at her room at the court house during the night time or any portion of the night during the period of your acquaintance.

A. Yes, sir.

Q. You may state who thus visited her?

A. Oscar Wilhite made a couple of trips.

Conveniently, according to Wilhite's testimony, Minnie's room, located on the second floor of the sheriff's house, was across the hall from the room he shared with Gutekunst. And since Minnie was treated as a family member who came and went as she wanted, her door was never locked.

Once sympathetic toward Minnie, many were outraged at her supposed seduction of the teenagers, forgetting that she was a teenager herself and even younger than both boys. People wrote letters—oh, did they write letters—including the following two, both published in the *Emporia Weekly News* on Thursday, December 24, 1885.

Minnie Again

Americus, Kansas. Mr. Editor: It is fast getting to be that Emporia is nothing if not sensational, and now comes the Widow Walkup about to add another sensation to the one so recently produced by her in your pleasant little city, but this time the sensation involves scandal, and bids fair to become brimful in more ways than one.

The problem to be solved in this case appears to be—how came the milk in the coconut—verily the Hotel de Wilhite must be an accommodating institution and to be well patronized. Up to the present, only two depositions have been made, and these have been sufficient to put public expectancy on the qui vive and it will be difficult to tell what the developments will be when all parties have been examined. That is my opinion at any rate.

"Poor, dear, innocent little Minnie!"

How many of us ladies were taken in and done by her childish face and her luminous eyes, her pouting lips and pearly teeth that made her the envy of her own sex. And then that poor old man, her guardian. Is it not fortunate that he was in New Orleans when the scandal went broadcast over the tell-tale wires in all its revelations of filth and indecency? It is to be hoped that his eyes may be spared the distressing perusal in the public prints. It is still more especially to be hoped that anyone who may write to him at 222 Canal Street, New Orleans may make no allusion to the dread particulars.

One does not see his idol ruthlessly shattered by a single blow without experiencing consequences more or less serious and nothing so thoroughly it affects the human heart as to see its acme of all virtues reduced in the twinkling of the bedpost to personifier of all vices.

Can such things be overcome as like a courthouse cloud? Yes, verily; and the end is not yet."

Country Lass.

Minnie, as usual, remained calm despite these damning allegations. Gutekunst had tried to blackmail her to keep from telling his lies, she said. Why Mit (Oscar Milton Wilhite) would say such things she had no idea. She also floated the idea that they were put up to it by her deceased's husband's heirs as part of their plot to keep her from inheriting his estate.

In keeping with her inability to remember inconvenient facts, Minnie denied saying she might be expecting despite having telling several reporters at the *Sharon News* just the opposite. The following ran in a story on October 28, 1885, "Mrs. Walker expects to become a mother ere long."

Minnie also didn't remember asking for an extra portion of Walkup's insurance. The four beneficiaries—Minnie and Walkup's three children—were each to receive $2,000. If Minnie was pregnant with Walkup's child, she would have received a larger share.

Whether Minnie slept with the two young men conveniently located across the hall in hopes of getting pregnant with a child she could pass off as Walkup's (remember there was no DNA testing back then) or that Mit and Edward had lied became moot. No child arrived, and the two men later recanted their stories, though they never explained why they made their accusations in the first place.

Minnie fans will be happy to know crime does pay, and in Minnie's case it paid quite well. She inherited $250,000 (approximately $6 million today) from the estate and $4,000 of Walkup's insurance. Minnie was definitely rich and single again.

Next in Line?

Senator Kellogg began his career as a carpetbagger, moving from Illinois to Louisiana after the Civil War, where he was appointed governor by President Ulysses Grant. In his short tenure, he managed to earn a less than stellar reputation and was considered to be one of the most corrupt politicians in the state—which in Louisiana at that time was a very high bar to reach.

Born on December 8, 1830, Kellogg was old, old, old compared to Minnie, but also exceedingly rich—he was another prime example that crime certainly does pay. He helped Minnie squeeze the Walkup estate for even more money. She had just returned from a trip to Europe, accompanied by her mother—and possibly Kellogg, who was between US Senate terms—when the papers reported she'd been awarded Walkup's Civil War pension. According to reporters, ex-governor William Pitt Kellogg was "accredited with the honor of having influenced the granting of the pension."

All in all, Minnie's take from Walkup was worth a fortune. Not bad for a marriage that lasted just one month.

Classic Minnie

Newspapers across the nation tracked Minnie and Kellogg's cross-country railroad trip.

One stop was in Newton, Kansas, where she was met by the Honorable William Jay, her former guardian, and his wife. Together they traveled to Emporia, where Minnie had business regarding Walkup's estate. The Jays also questioned Minnie's relationship with the senator.

There was nothing between them, Minnie said, growing heated at the thought that anyone could think otherwise. The fact was, she told newsmen and the Jays, Senator Kellogg and his sister were her companions on the trip. For some odd reason Kellogg's sister's name never appeared on any of the travel manifests which pesky reporters were quick to point out. (We're thinking it must have been a clerical error on the part of the railroad and hotels.)

Minnie then played the father/uncle card, saying she'd known the senator since childhood and he'd always taken a fatherly interest in her. Working herself up into a dignified huff of respectability, she described herself annoyed beyond expression by the vile slanders upon herself and her honored friend.

The senator and the widow traveled all over, taking the Dallas and Pacific from New Orleans to El Paso, where Kellogg was to look after some business he had in Texas and Pacific land-grant bonds. That man had his hands in everything.

When they arrived in Chicago, Kellogg checked into a hotel, and, as the Chicago papers reported, a lady who arrived at the same time registered as Mrs. M. A. Wallace. She didn't fool anyone.

It was duly noted that Wallace and Kellogg went out riding during their stay. Later, they both left town on the same train. Another coincidence, of course.

By the way, there was no record of Mr. Kellogg's sister checking into the hotel.

Peering into the Future

Toward the turn of the twentieth century, when another husband died and Minnie inherited another fortune, one snide reporter, writing for the Thursday, November 18, 1897, edition of the *Vicksburg Evening Post*, noted that Minnie was very fond of high living and notoriety—the kind that happens when you go on trips with Willie Kellogg, one-time governor of Louisiana during Reconstruction and subsequently a United States senator from that state for ten years.

"Willie, we are quite sure," wrote the reporter, "will be very happy to hear that Minnie has come into the possession of a handsome fortune and very probably will tender his distinguished services in helping her to spend it."

The prescient reporter, seemingly knowing his subject quite well, said that despite her large inheritance from husband number two, Minnie would quickly spend it all and then would doubtlessly "infatuate and marry some other old fool with money."

So she would, and now it's time for us to move on to the next stage of Minnie's life.

Canal Street, where Elizabeth Wallace ran a "boardinghouse,"
in the 1880s. *Photo courtesy of the Library of Congress, Prints
& Photographs Division, Detroit Publishing Company Collection
[reproduction number, LC-DIG-det-4a26981].*

WORLD'S INDUSTRIAL & COTTON CENTENNIAL EXPOSITION AT NEW ORLEANS. LA.

HORTICULTURAL HALL.

DIMENSIONS, SIX HUNDRED BY ONE HUNDRED & NINETY FOUR FEET.

CENTRE ARRANGED TO SHOW 20,000 PLATES OF FRUIT.

The World's International and Cotton Centennial Exposition, held from December 1, 1884, to May 31, 1885, attracted visitors from around the world, including politician and businessman James Walkup, who traveled from Emporia, Kansas. *Photo courtesy of the Library of Congress, Prints and Photographs Division [reproduction number, LC-DIG-pga-01657].*

SHARP SHOOTING.

A Brisk Fusilade in the Mascot Office.

Jas. D. Houston and Robert Brewster Go In to Give its Editor a Clubbing — They Make Their Exit Wounded,

The Former in His Right Hand, the Latter with Four Holes in His Body.

Brewster's Wounds Regarded as Fatal— George Osmond, of the Mascot, also Wounded.

Camp street at noon yesterday, as it was a very bright, pleasant day, was crowded with

Minnie wasn't the only femme fatale in the Wallace family. Her older half sister Dora, though married and very pregnant, was often seen with Judge William Houston, which inspired a shooting at the *Mascot*, a newspaper that specialized in criticizing the rich and powerful. *Photo courtesy of Sally Asher.*

Trying to decide whether to marry James Walkup, Minnie and her mother toured Emporia, Kansas, to see if James Walkup was as wealthy as he said he was. *Photo courtesy of the* Chicago Daily Tribune, *Sunday, December 26, 1897.*

An invitation to the exclusive Rex Ball, circa 1880.
Photo courtesy of Digital History Online.

Josephine Moffitt, one of Minnie's good friends in Chicago. She and Minnie most likely knew each other in New Orleans, as they were born four days apart and both attended the same convent school. *Photo courtesy of the Library of Congress, Prints and Photographs Division [reproduction number, LC-DIG-ggbain-00792].*

This newspaper illustration shows Minnie nursing her husband of less than a month as he lay dying from arsenic poison. *Photo courtesy of the* Chicago Daily Tribune, *Sunday, December 26, 1897.*

Minnie testifying in the Walkup murder trial. Her testimony was so moving that reporters said everyone, including the stenographer, cried. *Photo courtesy of the* Chicago Daily Tribune, *Sunday, December 26, 1897.*

After James Walkup died, Minnie first took a cross-country train trip with the very married ex-US senator William Pitt Kellogg, a carpetbagger who also had been governor of Louisiana. The couple then purportedly traveled to Europe together. *Photo courtesy of the* Chicago Daily Tribune, *Sunday, December 26, 1897.*

Prince Victor and Josephine pledging their troth over dinner in New York City. Unfortunately for Josephine, the prince had no intention of really marrying her and soon snuck out of the country. *Photo courtesy of the* Pittsburgh Press, *Sunday, December 11, 1921.*

Gladys Vanderbilt was rumored to be on Prince Victor's list of acceptable heiresses (anyone with a fortune under $2 million need not apply), but Count László Széchenyi, a Hungarian aristocrat, got her instead. Here is the couple with Alice Roosevelt Longworth at the dedication of the Lincoln Memorial. *Photo courtesy of the Library of Congress, Prints and Photographs Division [reproduction number, LC-USZ62–110538].*

One of the notes and letters Josephine presented in court to try to convince the judge she was indeed the common-law wife of the prince. It didn't work. *Photo courtesy of the* Pittsburgh Press, *Sunday, December 11, 1921.*

After marrying Prince Victor, Lida sued Josephine Moffitt, who was also calling herself the princess of Thurn and Taxis. Lida won, but that didn't stop Josephine from using the title, at least for a while. *Photo courtesy of the Pennsylvania Room at the Uniontown Public Library.*

Lida Fitzgerald with her three sons by her first marriage. She would later sue John in an attempt to void his marriage. It was one of the few of the lawsuits that she lost. *Photo courtesy of the Pennsylvania Room at the Uniontown Public Library.*

Lida with her second husband, Prince Victor Thurn and Taxis, and her son John. By the next year, the prince would be dead and Lida would go to court, trying to keep the Polish dancer he was courting from inheriting his small fortune. *Photo courtesy of the Pennsylvania Room at the Uniontown Public Library.*

An illustrator's rendition of the fateful first meeting between Minnie and her second husband, John B. Ketcham, another rich, older man. *Photo courtesy of the Pennsylvania Room at the Uniontown Public Library.*

The Boody House, where Ketcham and his second wife,
Nettie Poe, the Belle of Toledo, lived before they moved to Chicago.
*Photo courtesy of the Library of Congress, Prints & Photographs
Division, Detroit Publishing Company Collection [reproduction
number, LC-DIG-det-4a23281].*

Minnie went to Dethlef Hansen for help in avoiding paying her bills. The two got along so well that Hansen helped her get Ketcham's fortune. He then moved into her home. *Photo courtesy of the* Chicago Daily Tribune, *Sunday, December 26, 1897.*

Butler Joseph Keller would be a witness in John Ketcham's signing of the will that left his entire fortune to Minnie. Even more so, many wondered if Keller had been a stand-in for the groom when she purportedly married Ketcham in Milwaukee. *Photo courtesy of the* Chicago Daily Tribune, *Sunday, December 26, 1897.*

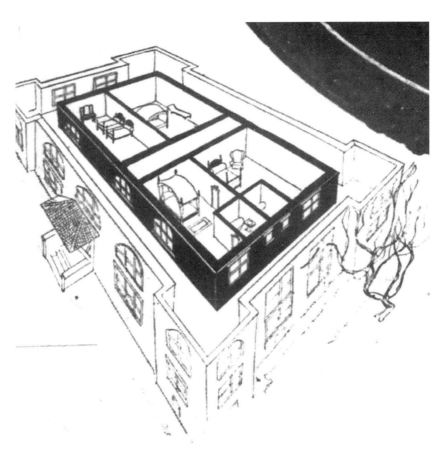

The house within a house that DeLancy Louderback built at a cost of $1 million and then furnished for another $1 million for Minnie. When she refused to move in after it was completed, he set her up in a fancy apartment in New York City. *Photo courtesy of the* Washington (DC) Times, *Sunday, August 25, 1918.*

In 1914, Minnie made the papers again when DeLancy Louderback died from ingesting cyanamide and left her a part of his estate. *Photo courtesy of the* Washington (DC) Times, *Sunday, August 25, 1918.*

Minnie's death certificate. She died in San Diego on May 10, 1957, and is buried without a headstone. *Photo courtesy of Jane Simon Ammeson.*

ſ

BLOOD MONEY SQUANDERED

The Necessity of Catching Mr. Ketcham

NOTHING LASTS FOREVER, NOT EVEN MONEY INHERITED from a murdered husband and funds provided by enamored older men. After touring Europe with her mother and Senator Kellogg (where, we keep asking, was his wife?), Minnie's funds were precariously low. It's important to stop here a moment and consider this. Six years earlier, after the Walkup estate was settled, Minnie inherited around $250,000—just a little less than $6 million in today's money. In early 1892, she was so broke she couldn't pay a clothing bill for around $600 ($15,246) owed to a store in New Orleans. Faced with this dire situation, Minnie hired an auctioneering house to sell off her possessions.

Most Extraordinary Sale

Superbly Furnished Residence
MRS. MINNIE WALLACE WALKUP,
NO. 244 CANAL STREET.
Times-Picayune, Sunday, April 17, 1892

The handsomest collection of Household Effects offered to the public in several years, in perfect order and scarcely six months in use.

An advertisement place in the newspaper by Onorato & Stuart, Auctioneers, for a sale of Minnie's entire household included such items as (prices in brackets are 2016 dollars):

· One Beautiful Sevres China Jardinière, cost $100 [$2,500] in Paris.
· Elegant Walnut Hatrack cost $100 [$2,500].
· One Exquisite Bedroom Set, in bamboo, very beautifully finished, $800 [$20,328.81].
· One Magnificent Venice Martin Cabinet, Onyx Finish Cost $50 [$1,270].
· Elegant B. Mantel Mirrors Cost $300 [$7,600].
· One Superb Washstand Set, Cost $50 [$1,270].
· Rich and Artistic Marble Bust "Frivolity" Cost $75 [$19.05].
· Six or Eight Magnificent Bedroom Sets
· Handsome Chairs.
· Water Colors.
· Oil Paintings
· Etchings
· Engravings
· Toilet Sets
· Magnificent Mantel Cabinets
· Beautiful Brussels Carpet and Rugs
· Cut Crystal Candelabra
· Magnificent Upright Plane Exquisite Parlor Furniture
· Beautiful Antique Oak Étagère
· Superb Bric-a-Brac in Royal Worcester, Dresden, Carlsbad, Doulton and Minton
· A Handsome Oil Painting of a Famous Beauty
· Magnificent Dining-room Furniture in Oak
· Elegant Silk Curtains and Draperies
· A Magnificent Upright Piano
· Exquisite Parlor Furniture
· Rugs. Mattings, etc. and thousands of very beautiful things, too numerous to mention.
Terms Cash before delivery.
No admittance to residence until day of sale.

The sale was originally scheduled for Thursday, April 21, 1892, at eleven o'clock in the morning. But on Friday, April 22, 1892, an advertisement in the *Times-Picayune* stated the sale would absolutely take place that morning, "regardless of weather."

Of course, Minnie selling her possessions made national news and again brought up the tale of her murdered husband. It also caused rampant speculation as to what Minnie was up to, as shown in this snide article that ran in several Kansas and Missouri newsletters.

Why This Public Sale?
Mrs. Minnie Wallace-Walkup's Costly Furniture Going at Auction
Sedalia (MO) Weekly Bazoo, Tuesday, April 26, 1892

In 1884 Minnie Wallace, a pretty brunette living at 222 Canal St., New Orleans, left a handsome southern home to cast her fortune with a man whose name afterwards brought her into great prominence. When Minnie Wallace-Walkup appeared in Cincinnati on her bridal tour, the most expert charges of feminine beauty were all of the opinion that the pretty bride had easily seen 23 summers. When, however, some months afterwards she was arraigned in court at her home in Emporia Kansas, on the charge of administering poison and to the husband from whom she expected great wealth, the records in her native country, to the amazement of all, said that she was only 18 years old years of age [sic]. Upon the plea of extreme youth some eccentric people espoused Mrs. Walkup's case in Emporia and the jury failed to say that Mrs. Walker poisoned her husband.

The story is widely known. Canal Street, now made famous by the intrigues of the pretty miss who is held in high esteem by southern gentlemen, once more became her home. Here she refused to see any of the friends who claimed to be her acquaintance from her quondam northern home. Her home on Canal Street was furnished and finished in all the elegance becoming the style of Southern legislators and planters, whose company she entertained with the same grace and charm which only a comparatively short time before had captivated an apparently good catch of a husband.

That her home after her return to New Orleans was all that wealth and luxury could desire is shown in a notice of sale, which appears in the New Orleans Picayune, under date of April 21st.

In prominent lines a most extraordinary sale is announced. The entire contents of the superbly furnished residence of Mrs. Minnie Wallace-Walkup, being the handsomest collection of household effects submitted to the public in several years, are offered to the public in several years, are offered at public auction to the highest bidder.

The bill of sale enumerates articles of furniture rich, rare and costly, with pieces of art in painting and statuary, which would reflect credit upon the taste of the most opulent.

But now the query occurs to those of her Northern friends who knew her so well: Why would Minnie thus so summarily dispose of such a cozy and artistic home? Surely ill fortune could not fall to the lot of such a beauty.

But perhaps she intends a second time to seek happiness in a second marriage. The latter seems to be the most probable.

As the paper insinuated, she was most likely on the move, this time to Chicago.

Reverting to her maiden name—and at times using Estelle or Estella as her first name—sometime after the sale, she and her mother first moved to 1401 Michigan Avenue (where her future friends—the most notorious Josephine and Gladys Forbes lived) in Chicago and then to a stately home at 3421 Indiana Avenue in what was then a very fashionable neighborhood south of Chicago's Loop. Many thought that Minnie's avuncular travel companion, the senator, had paid for the home and its furnishings. The neighborhood, which fell on hard times in the mid-twentieth century, is once again seeing its fortunes rise, but unfortunately, Minnie's home has been torn down in a block where new homes and renovated late nineteenth-century brownstones are making the area desirable again. It would be great to be able to ring the doorbell and walk through the rooms where so much was about to happen in Minnie's life. Alas, we'll have to just recount the events, starting with Minnie's recollection years later of her meeting with her next husband, John Borden Ketcham, who after meeting and wooing Minnie would come to a suspicious end, but only after he had signed his own death warrant (also known as his last will and testament).

Minnie waxed eloquent to a reporter years later that she moved to Chicago because she desired to revive her spirits and thought the large, bustling city offered both a chance for a quiet life and the restorative actions that new sights would bring to her. She said she refused offers to go on stage, though some said she had asked to do so and was turned down. She also took up literary works. Her book, *Driftwood: Sketches in Poetry and Prose*, is still available as a free e-book on Google and can also be bought online. We didn't buy it, but we read a few pages online so you wouldn't have to.

Here's an example: "She did not finish the sentence. The little heart fluttered a moment, the weak arms clasped about his neck and as the eyes closed the gentled head sank upon his bosom and the soul of the girl went out of the house of clay, just as a bit of golden sun crept in the blinds and fell upon them both."

Minnie quickly fell in with a fast set of women known for their beauty as well as their enjoyment of late nights, champagne, rich men, and scandalous behavior. Beautifully dressed and lovely to look at, she attracted attention as she moved through the demimonde of Chicago, frequenting places in or near the Levee, the notorious red-light district where rich men, both young and old, rubbed shoulders with working men in search of pleasure. There were places in the Levee where a man could get his needs met for very little sums indeed. But for the clubmen with money to burn, several places, including the Monroe restaurant, run by Gladys Forbes, were a step above, say, Frank Wing's, where a guy could, and sometimes did, get killed or at least be forced to stay until his money was all spent. Forbes liked to facilitate relationships, and when gentlemen walked into at her place, she'd call some girlfriends and invite them to stop by. If things worked out, Gladys probably made a small commission; plus, it encouraged other well-to-do gentlemen to frequent her place. Consider Gladys a matchmaker (or, as the less lofty might call her, a pimp) but also a marketer.

The ultimate bordello belonged to two enterprising sisters, Minnie and Ada Simms, who went by the last name of Everleigh and whose opulent home was known as the Everleigh Club. While Minnie Everleigh and her sister Ada didn't open their place until 1900, our Minnie had her own secret place at 2281 Indiana that she paid sixteen dollars a month for and rented under the name Kellard or Kelly. Neighbors noted a lot of liquor being delivered. But Minnie, like the Everleigh sisters, was all about class—fine wines, gourmet food, refined conversation in a well-appointed setting. Minnie Walkup was the only woman in attendance so it wasn't a well-established bordello like the Everleigh Club, where the Everleigh sisters took a commission from the services their girls provided. Minnie's business model was more direct. Unfortunately for her, though she took in great amounts of cash, she spent even more.

So here was Minnie in Chicago, beautiful and broke.

Think of it as déjà vu all over again. Like the Cotton Exposition in New Orleans in 1885, a great influx of people arrived in the city for the 1893 World's Columbia Exposition. Also known as the Chicago World's Fair and the Chicago Columbian Exposition, the event celebrating the four hundredth anniversary of Christopher Columbus's landing in the New World in 1492 and was an extravaganza of new technology, including the first Ferris wheel and the first moving walkway, called a travelator. Covering 630 acres on Chicago's Lakefront, parks, lagoons, and canals were created, and two hundred "temporary" buildings made of granite in the neoclassical architecture style were constructed. Only two of these still stand—the Field Museum and the Museum of Science and Industry. Three million people attended, coming from more than forty-six countries. It would be the perfect hunting ground for a man killer like Minnie. Only she didn't need any of those three million. Her next victim was already there, having moved from Toledo with his wife just a few years earlier. Yes, dear readers, he was married, but that was no impediment to Minnie's plans.

So let us meet husband number two.

"I was introduced to Mr. Ketcham by a man who believed, as he said afterwards, that I might put some happiness into Mr.

Ketcham's life," wrote Minnie in the *Chicago Tribune* account of her life. "When I finally learned of his having a wife it was at a time when the greatest sorrow had come into my life. She who had with gentle care guided me for years was no more. Mr. Ketcham explained to me that he had kept from telling me the truth, knowing that I would be refuse to see him again. Soon after followed his divorce and then he insisted upon marrying me the next day."

Let's sort out fact from fiction here. Yes, Elizabeth Wallace did die. Minnie purchased two plots in Forest Home Cemetery, and Elizabeth rests there. For some reason neither Minnie nor Dora purchased a headstone for their mother—maybe money was tight. And Minnie wouldn't buy a tombstone for Dora either when she died in 1921.

So, yes, Minnie was telling the truth about the passing of her mother, so we'll give her credit for the veracity of that part of her story. Now, as for the rest.

Do any of the readers out there believe that Minnie would never have consorted with a married man? If they do, let us remind them of Senator Kellogg, who somewhere had a wife, though little is ever of heard of her—let's hope she had her own happy diversions. Recall also Mr. Jay, Judge Houston, and Lord knows who else. So forgive us for being just a little hesitant to believe that innocent Minnie didn't know that Ketcham—a noted man about town whose second wife, Nettie Poe, appeared at many high society events—was married. But that was Minnie's story, and she was sticking to it.

The Future Groom and His Current Wife

John Berdan Ketcham was born into a wealthy and prominent family in Toledo, Ohio. His father, Valentine H. Ketcham of Toledo, was credited with founding the city and at the time of his death in 1887 was one of the wealthiest men in Toledo, leaving an estate valued at $5 million (some accounts say it was $10 million). Valentine and his wife, Rachel, née Berdan, had three sons—George Henry, John Berdan, and Valentine Hicks—and a daughter, Mary Elizabeth.

Though he'd later fritter away a vast fortune, to begin with John Ketcham was not a slacker sponging off his wealthy parents. He was an astute businessman and prior to the death of his father, he'd proven himself so by organizing the bank of J. B. Ketcham & Co. in Toledo, which later became the Ketcham National Bank.

John married Mary Etta Granger on January 8, 1874. After Granger died in 1884, Ketcham went on to marry twenty-year-old Nettie Poe. Their marriage, which took place on October 22, 1885, was described as brilliant. Nettie, vivacious, handsome, and finely educated, was a brilliant hostess. In her obituary, Nettie and John were described as leaders of the gay social life that defined Toledo in the early 1880s and 1890s. They lived in a suite of rooms at the Boody House hotel, which opened in June 1872. Fabulously swanky, each of its 133 guest rooms had its own fireplace as well as hot and cold running water—a very big deal back then.

Their home, decorated with treasures brought from every corner of Europe, became the mecca for the best people of Toledo. They traveled extensively. Their stables were filled with the best horses and carriages that could be bought. The couple glittered atop Toledo's social hierarchy.

In other words, they were the late nineteenth-century equivalent of a power couple.

But then Ketcham decided to up his game, startling Toledo by announcing he was going to dispose of his controlling share in the bank he founded and move to Chicago. Their magnificent establishment—like a palace, as the papers described it—was closed, and the couple left Toledo for Chicago. Their new digs? The Lexington Hotel located at 2135 S. Michigan Avenue, which had been built in 1892 for attendees of the 1893 Columbus Exposition. Sumptuous to extreme, the Ketchams paid $1,000 ($25,500) a month for their rooms there.

They had, as one newsman put it, more money than anybody.

That is until John met Minnie, the great separator of a man and his money.

Not that John needed help. He was morphing from a hard-driven businessman who enjoyed a whirlwind social life to a man who drank and spent too much.

The Pace That Kills

Was Traveled by Mr. Ketcham of Chicago
A Life That Might Have Been Useful and Valuable Was Wasted.
A Decidedly Fast Class.
Was the One in Which He Entered,
And as the Husband of Minnie Wallace Walkup He Lost.

Hutchinson (KS) News, Wednesday, November 17, 1897

Having moved to Chicago, Ketcham didn't settle into the routine of contented married life. Being in a new city seemed to demand of him a new life, one not encumbered by a wife. "It was subsequent to this that shadows fell in the path of his married life" was how the *Chicago Daily Tribune* described what happened to the Ketcham marriage after the move. Dark shadows, indeed. Ketcham quickly became well known as a "clubman" among Chicago's fast-living set. He moved out of the Lexington Hotel and took rooms at the eleven-story Auditorium Annex. Lest you think poor John was moving into the equivalent of a single room at the YMCA, let us reassure you. The elaborately designed, eleven-story hotel (now the Congress Plaza), was an addition to the Auditorium Hotel, on Michigan Avenue. Built in 1893 and popular for its private baths, it was a favorite of Chicago's captains of industry, society, politics, and culture, as well as the many visitors coming to the city to attend the World's Columbian Exposition. Among its many stunning architectural flourishes was "Peacock Alley," an underground marble passageway connecting the annex to the Auditorium Hotel, which had been designed by Louis Sullivan.

With Nettie still living at the Lexington, Ketcham was free to enjoy the activities in life he loved, owning and betting on horses, overindulging in rich foods and alcohol, and carousing with beautiful women, including our own Minnie.

Before we continue with the fairytale union of Minnie and John, let's take a moment to see what Ketcham was trading in for his newer, slightly younger model.

The Second Mrs. Ketcham

Nettie, who was educated in a convent school (just like Minnie), was said to be among the most beautiful and brilliant women of her time, earning the nickname "Belle of Toledo," according to Barbara Johnson writing *In Search of Our Past: Women of North-west Ohio, Volume II* (Toledo, OH: Women's History Committee of the Women Alive! Coalition, 1990), which is posted on the Poe family's Ancestry.com page.

Her father, a cousin of poet Edgar Allan Poe, was a real estate developer and also assisted Toledo's growth through more than three decades as a director of the Toledo Savings Bank & Trust. Nettie's mother helped incorporate and was an officer of the Protestant Hospital, which later became the Toledo Hospital. She was serving as the hospital's president when she died in 1890.

Nettie was twenty when she married John in October 1885, which intriguingly is about the time sixteen-year-old Minnie was on trial for murdering James Walkup. We know Minnie was made of strong stuff, but so was Nettie. A telling anecdote about her is found in her obituary.

> One day in the late 1880s, Nettie was driving a two-wheel dog cart with horses hitched in tandem and a groom seated in the back. The dogcart was well remembered by two 14-year-old boys who have never seen the likes of such a cart before and were struck by Nettie's beauty describing her as a "fairy princess."
>
> Nettie was driving down Madison Avenue, one of the few cedar-paved streets in Toledo at that time, when the boys watching yelled a warning. One of the horses reared, upsetting the dogcart, tumbling the groom off the back and throwing Nettie to the pavement. As the boys calmed the horses, Nettie picked herself up and thanked the boys before getting back into the cart to drive home to the Boody House alone since the groom refused to board the cart again.

Think about this—a rich, possibly (or, more likely, probably) pampered, wealthy, and gorgeous woman of excellent pedigree gets thrown out of a dog cart. Brushing herself off, she climbs back in, something her groom is unwilling to do. This is a woman who wasn't going to pine for a straying husband. While other wives had suffered while their men wooed Minnie—we're looking at you, Mrs. Kellogg, Mrs. Houston, Mrs. Jay, and in the future, Mrs. De Lancy Louderback, who fled a ball crying when her husband became enraptured upon spying Minnie, adorned in peacock feathers, for the first time across a crowded room— Nettie Poe Ketcham, the daughter of a wealthy early founder of the city of Toledo and first cousin once removed of Edgar Allan Poe, wasn't one of those wives. Knowing about her husband's romance, she decided to cut bait. Another deciding factor may have been that his friends were already suggesting a conservator be appointed to manage his finances.

Nettie was one smart cookie because by the time she got her divorce, the once vibrant, successful, and wealthy Ketcham was turning into a drunken lout who was quickly dissipating his fortune, a good deal of it on gifts and cash given to the expensive Minnie.

A Chicago Judge Takes the Record for Quick
Severing of the Conjugal Knot
Happy Ending of One Woman's Drama
Logansport (IN) Pharos-Tribune, Sunday, November 15, 1896.

Seldom has a decree of divorce given rise to so much criticism and comment as Judge Payne's record breaker in Chicago the other day in which he released Nettie Poe Ketcham from the bonds that bound her in matrimony to John B. Ketcham, the millionaire son of Toledo's late multimillionaire banker. Unprecedented in the history of Cook County divorce court was the action of the well-known jurist and the manner in which the proceedings were hurried through fairly took the breath of all who witnessed them. The bill was filed at 2 o'clock and 20 minutes later Mrs. Ketcham hurried out of the room a free woman.

In the morning the question of an appointment of a conservator for John Ketcham came up on a petition before Judge

Kohlsant. The case was continued. At 3 o'clock a bill for divorce was filed with the clerk of the superior court and an immediate hearing was had which resulted in the decree being granted. The bill was exceedingly brief containing but one page into charges both of drunkenness and infidelity.

Although John Ketcham's attorneys were in the courtroom, none of the witnesses were cross-examined. Both John and Nettie wanted to call it quits and had already negotiated a settlement. Nettie's haul: $150,000 (today, a little over $4 million), the right to rid herself not only of the man but also of his last name, and, best of all, her self-respect.

Following the divorce, the Belle of Toledo returned to her hometown, where she lived with her father. Following his death and that of Ketcham (you did know he was going to die, didn't you?), Nettie moved to New York City. Suffering the loss of her voice and unable to find a physician to help her, she traveled to see a specialist in Switzerland for help. She loved Switzerland so much that even when her voice returned, she decided to live there, visiting the homes of royalty and writing them letters of introduction when they traveled to the United States for the first time, remaining, even without her ex-husband, a certified power broker.

During World War I, Nettie stocked her home with sewing and knitting machines, producing clothing for those in need. She gave her limousine to the Swiss army to use as an ambulance and also donated large sums of money to equip Swiss hospitals during the war. When the war ended, Nettie settled in the village of Heimberg, Switzerland, where she visited the sick, taking them food and clothing, and supplied vitamins and orange juice to undernourished children. But she didn't forget Toledo either and made numerous donations to civic organizations there.

While Nettie was becoming a great philanthropist, Minnie would soon be battling her "in-laws" for Ketcham's money. But she had to marry him first and get him to sign a will leaving his money to her. That seems to have been somewhat more difficult than expected.

6

THE IMPORTANCE OF KEEPING MR. KETCHAM— AND HIS MONEY

CAPTIVATING KETCHAM PROVED TO BE AN EASIER TASK for Minnie than getting him to marry her. After the divorce, Ketcham remained at the Annex instead of moving in with Minnie. It could be he'd developed cold feet about marrying for a third time. Maybe he liked his freedom. Maybe he knew what had happened to J. R. Walkup after he walked down the aisle.

Ketcham continued drinking and frittering away his money, and though Minnie was often at his side, so were other women as well. There was a chance he could slip from her grasp if some equally conniving female chose to capture him. But then, there was no equally conniving woman like our Minnie. Still she needed a plan if she wanted to marry Ketcham and gain access to his money.

And, of course, Minnie being Minnie, she did have a plan.

Ketcham's comings and goings at the Annex were so erratic, and because his belongings were still in his room, at first both the staff and his friends didn't notice he hadn't been there in a long time. He wouldn't be coming back either. Minnie had taken control and installed him in her Indiana Avenue home. Talk about spider and the fly.

For the first eight months of his last illness, he was wheeled around Indiana Avenue in an invalid's chair, but then he disappeared inside her home, too ill to receive visitors or to go out, she told people. Doctors were in attendance, but it was Minnie who had charge of the sickroom and was the one to administer all his medications. Helping her imprison Walkup were Joe Keller, the butler, and her attorney, Hansen. Both played a large part in the next phase of the scam.

Ketcham's family back in Toledo were worried, and his brother George traveled to Chicago, wanting to take him back home. No way, said Minnie. Worried and angered, Ketcham discussed the matter with Detective Herman, who told him it was impossible to do anything as long as John Ketcham was in his right mind and didn't want to leave. And so, George returned to Toledo without his brother.

On September 23, 1887, Minnie, Ketcham, and Joe Keller, the butler, boarded a train for Milwaukee and upon arrival checked into a hotel, where they spent the night. The next morning, Ketcham and Minnie went to the home of Reverend Mr. J. P. Roberts to be married; then, having been pronounced man and wife, they boarded the train with Kelly and returned to Chicago.

While He Lay Dying

Despite her protestations of love and her avowal of staying by his bedside day and night, Minnie had other men to keep enthralled with her charms. "Mrs. Ketcham's time was not entirely taken up with her home and husband at No. 3421 Indiana Avenue," a reporter snidely wrote in the November 17, 1897, issue of *The World*, a New York newspaper. "Long before she married, she rented a flat at No. 2233 Indiana Avenue under the name of Mrs. Keller, and there entertained friends in princely style. Neighbors who saw Mrs. Keller say she and Mrs. Ketcham are one."

Dr. Minnie Ministers to a Dying Husband Again

The two physicians attending him, Dr. Kiernan and Dr. Deveney, tried to stop his drinking. Minnie had a different take on how to treat a sick alcoholic. The doctors would later testify that she often smuggled liquor into Ketcham's sick room, resulting in his being in a drunken stupor most of the time. When confronted with her behavior, Mrs. Ketcham said it was necessary to supply him with liquor to keep him alive.

Unfortunately her medical ministrations didn't work—or perhaps they did.

Another One Bites the Dust

Newspapers reported the death of prominent millionaire John B. Ketcham at 3421 Indiana Avenue. Minnie made sure to tell reporters immediately that not only was she the widow of the deceased, having married him September 24, but also his entire fortune had been left to her according to his last will.

It was a surprise, as one news reporter drily put it: "Friends and relatives of Mr. Ketcham, when told last night of the circumstances of his death, expressed surprise to learn of his recent conjugal experience."

Ketcham's family learned about his death through an Associated Press dispatch someone showed to them. Minnie denied not notifying the family, saying she had sent a telegram. Whoever submitted the obituary that ran in the Chicago papers misstated the day of his death, writing Sunday instead of Saturday. Obviously, the poor widow was so overwhelmed she forgot about these minor details. She did not forget to let the world know she was devastated, an important fact she had forgotten after the death of Mr. Walkup, when she spent more time visiting and sewing her widow's gown.

The Grieving Widow Redux

All day Mrs. Ketcham sat in her front room upstairs, with tears coursing from under her black eyelids, she saw the neighbors for a block in either direction watching her house from their front windows and noted the arrival of the polis and the Coroner's deputies. When she was plied with questions about her acquaintance and marriage with Ketcham she answered them all and was corroborated in everything regarding the will by the attorney who had drawn it up, Dethlef C. Hansen. Mrs. Ketcham's cousin, a Mrs. Torrey, who, with the butler, witnessed the will, refused to answer any questions.

—*The Milwaukee Journal*, November 18, 1897

Have we mentioned that Mrs. Sena Torrey was Elizabeth Wallace's cousin? Just a coincidence, we're sure.

Though Minnie tried to keep her first marriage a secret, nosy news reporters soon found out.

Mrs. Ketchum [*sic*] Number three has lived at 3421 Indiana Ave. for three years and has been known among her neighbors as Mrs. Mabel Wallace, a widow of J. Wallace. She is really the widow of James R. Walkup of Emporia Kansas from whom she inherited 400,000. She was arrested for his murder by poison but was acquitted.

—*Toledo Blade*, November 18, 1897

The initial coroner's inquest showed Ketcham's death to be the result of acute alcoholism. George Ketcham wanted his brother's body shipped back to Toledo, but Minnie had already chosen Chicago's Forest Hill Cemetery as the place for interment. George won that battle after Minnie made him agree not to autopsy the brain.

Would You Believe There Was Strychnine Again?
Goes Over Three Days
Ketcham Inquest Postponed Until Next Monday
Dr. Noel Not Yet Ready to Report on the Result of
His Investigations—Autopsy of the Stomach Reveals
Traces of Strychnine—Prescriptions Prepared for
the Man Before His Death Under Consideration

—*Chicago Tribune*, November 20, 1897

Mrs. Ketcham Wins One Strong Point
The Widow Bitterly Declares That Her Husband's
Friends Were His Worst Enemies
New York Journal and Advertiser, November 23, 1897

"You did not fear the result of the analysis that was made on behalf of the coroner?" Mrs. Ketcham was asked. "Not in the slightest. I knew it would be a vindication for me. I have not seen the chemist's report, but have no doubt they found traces of strychnine, for Mr. Ketcham's physician has said it was one of the ingredients used in the prescriptions."

All we can say is, really Minnie, isn't that just a tad too obvious? But fortunately for our Black Widow, the coroner decided the amount of strychnine administered was not enough to have caused Ketcham's death.

Minnie's Memory Fails Again

As she had in Emporia, when she couldn't remember why she had purchased poison or even if she had, Minnie's amnesia reoccurred when questioned about her marriage to Ketcham.

Minnie at first told Ketcham's family she couldn't remember the name of the minister in Milwaukee who had married them but that it was no matter; the entire estate belonged to her. She had a will to prove it but didn't show it, saying it was locked away.

As for why they married in secret, we'll let Minnie tell it in her own words:

> Knowing Mr. Ketcham's weakness about drink I delayed our marriage from time to time, hoping for my sake he would stop drinking. He returned from a trip last August and insisted that I must keep my promise this time. I explained to him frankly that I dreaded the notoriety that a wedding would bring upon us. I shrank from the comments of the papers about my Kansas experience in his recent divorce. He argued that it was our business and ours alone. I argued that would be better to wait and be married abroad. Finally, he became ill, and each day would say: To prove my gratitude for all the tenderness you have shown me and in justice to yourself let's be married quietly in Milwaukee, and as there is no license needed there and we are strangers there our marriage will not be commented on.

The evening of September 23rd we reached Milwaukee; the morning of the 24th we were married. We discussed and argued about it so often that it should not have seemed strange, still I had my conflicting emotions. I suggested to Mr. Ketcham that as we were going very shortly to take a trip abroad that his physician had recommended we tell no one of our marriage. However, on our return to the hotel he told Keller, his valet, of our morning trip. Mr. Ketcham was very lovable. In all the disgrace that has been thrust upon me, the brave man who died in my arms, will live in my memory to console me and make me brave.

There were certain discrepancies in her story.

Tom Riley, the hackman who drove the couple to the reverend's house, said the man accompanying Mrs. Walkup was a foot shorter than Ketcham who stood at five feet, ten inches. Anna Miersch, who witnessed the ceremony, supported Riley's testimony. She remembered thinking, "What a little man to marry such a large, fine-looking woman." Mrs. W. A. Hunsberger, who also saw the couple, agreed.

Was He Ketcham? That's What Everyone Wanted to Know

The Ketchams weren't about to just hand over the cash, and after much ado, Minnie finally produced the documents. But if Minnie had hoped all would run smoothly, she was wrong. Soon reporters and the Ketcham family began asking if Joe Keller, the butler, had taken Ketcham's place at the altar.

If that sounds at all ridiculous, consider these questions, as we're sure the Ketcham family did. Why didn't John Ketcham tell his family he was married? Why go all the way to Milwaukee, particularly with Ketcham so ill he hadn't left the house in months? And why was the groom so swaddled in blankets that it was almost impossible to see his face, and yet the minister said he looked more like Keller than Ketcham? And why did the groom sport a mustache when Ketcham was clean shaven? Keller, it should be said, had a mustache.

If Ketcham was dying, as he surely was under Minnie's care, she needed to marry him before he passed away. Having Keller pretend to be Ketcham certainly made sense.

The newspapers and Ketcham's family were all over it.

Mrs. Walkup's Version
Tells About Her Milwaukee Marriages
(Ottawa, KS) Evening Herald, Friday, November 19, 1897

Keller told authorities that Ketcham's face was not wrapped up when he and Minnie set off to the minister's home. Reverend Roberts countered by saying the groom's face was partially muffled in a shawl but not enough to hide the mustache.

Did She Disguise a Man and Marry Him?
Milwaukee Journal, November 18, 1897

The death of John B. Ketcham, the clubman, in the apartment of Mabel Estelle Wallace, has developed into one of the strangest stories of a woman's meteoric career in Chicago's history. The woman, who is but 28 years old and widow of ex-Mayor John R. Walkup of Emporia, Kansas, is one of the most beautiful women in this city. She is claiming Ketcham's fortune on the ground of being his widow. Her butler, Joe Keller, has suddenly become an important factor.

Rev. Mr. Roberts of Milwaukee, who performed the ceremony, opens up rather startling possibilities by saying, when shown a photograph of Keller, that the picture much more resembles the man whom he married to Mrs. Walkup than does the picture of Mr. Ketcham.

As one would expect, Ketcham's brothers and sisters hired an attorney to contest two issues—whether there had been a marriage, and if there was a will, whether their sibling was sound of mind when he signed it.

Their attorney, James E. Purnell, said he had abundant proof that Ketcham was mentally unsound for almost a year prior to his death (indeed, he mentioned the word "insane" several times) and that Minnie hadn't offered any proof of their purported marriage. Purnell hired Chicago medical experts to remove and examine Ketcham's brain to be examined for signs of his intellectual capacity, even though George had promised no such thing would happen. But then lying to a liar doesn't count, does it?

James Purnell was one very busy lawyer. He received word that Minnie, who didn't attend her husband's funeral (she hadn't attended Walkup's either), had traveled to New York, where she negotiated the sale of $35,000 ($966,723.25) worth of bonds belonging to Ketcham, who held a large number of bonds in the Chicago Club, the New York Central Railroad, and the North Chicago Railway, as well as Toledo municipal bonds.

It was common, said friends of Ketcham, for him to carry bonds and coupons in his pockets, sometimes in amounts as large as $100,000 ($2.7 million) just as an ordinary person might stuff their pockets with letters and papers. It was a bold move on Minnie's part, but then such moves were her stock-in-trade.

Purnell was also looking for two men who had visited Ketcham on October 6, 1897, and found him to be dazed and incapable of understanding where he was. George told a reporter from *The World* that he'd visited his brother, who "seemed dazed," noting that perhaps his brain might not have been clear, as he was unable to understand the location of certain property and did not seem quite himself. Despite his brother's state, George said the two consumed two glasses of liquor together.

> The funeral of the late John B. Ketcham occurred at the home of his mother, Mrs. Rachel Ketcham. No. 200 South Madison street, at 3 o'clock this afternoon. The time had been set for an hour earlier, but was delayed an hour on account of the delay of his only sister, Mrs. Mars Searing, in arriving from New York, where she had been visiting. The services were conducted by Rev. W. W. Williams and were strictly private. The remains were placed in the vault at Wood-lawn cemetery and will be buried in the family vault. Today the employees of the Ketcham National bank sent a handsome floral tribute to the Ketcham residence, accompanied by an expressive memento of the past association with the deceased.
>
> —*(Chicago) Inter Ocean*, Thursday, November 18, 1897

Purnell and the authorities were closing in on Minnie, and uncharacteristically, she seemed to be succumbing to a state of nerves. Or, being Minnie, maybe she had just decided to engender a little sympathy as well as get a break from the police.

Mrs. Ketcham Is Prostrated
(Chicago) Inter Ocean, Thursday, November 18, 1897
Mrs. John Ketcham, formerly Mrs. Minnie Wallace, lay at her home, No. 3421 Indiana Avenue, yesterday suffering from nervous prostration, as the result of the sensational developments following her husband's death.

She was attended by Dr. De Veny [this is very similar to the spelling of Dr. Deveney, who was the attending physician for John Ketcham], her physician, who said that quiet and absolute rest were necessary if she was to be saved from a complete breakdown.

Although she appeared at first but little affected, the nervous strain of the last few days seriously told on her health, and no one is now allowed to see her but the nurse in charge and the physician.

While the young widow lay in a darkened room, attended by a motherly woman in soft slippers, the police at Thirty-Fifth Street station were kept busy answering questions about Joseph Keller."

The police had placed Keller in what the newspapers called a "sweat box" in an attempt to get him to tell the truth. Fortunately for the fortune huntress, Hansen managed to locate the missing butler. Keller had stuck to script and not revealed anything by the time Hansen arrived to demand his release. Later Hansen would get Reverend Roberts to change his story. Obviously, the fight for Ketcham's estate was in full force, and Minnie's attorney—and, at the time, good friend—was a champion at defending her cause.

Legal Points in the Case

Dethlef C. Hansen, Mrs. Ketcham's Attorney, Writes of Them
Chicago Tribune, Sunday, December 27, 1887

Mrs. John B. Ketcham's case from the beginning has been one continuous theatrical performance, largely consisting of tragedy, but occasionally intermixed with everything from melodrama to farce comedy. When the curtain falls on the final act the numerous villains that have so far appeared and any that may come upon the stage hereafter will have received their just dessert, as they generally do, to the entire satisfaction of the audience—which in this case is the public.

There has been nothing deep or mysterious about this case, and all the dark and sensational accusations made in certain quarters against a woman standing almost alone in the world are without the slightest foundation.

Is there anything strange about a man marrying a woman he loves, and then making a will leaving her his property? Why, then, all this sensation? It can be easily explained by using the old biblical quotation: "Where the carcasses be there shall the vultures be gathered together."

Four years later, in another courtroom, Minnie and Hansen would square off against each other, and her attorney in that case would contend that Hansen was an inept lawyer. But now he very forcefully argued that Minnie Wallace Walkup and John Ketcham were legally married and that the length of their marriage or the circumstances of it didn't matter. As for John's being insane, didn't the fact that he had the mental fitness to marry prove he was of sound mind?

Fortunately for Nettie Poe, who got out at the right time, but unluckily for the rest of the heirs, Ketcham had dissipated his vast fortune at a brisk rate. His estate, at the time of his death, had dwindled to around $175,000 ($4.8 million) according to one newspaper story. He'd lost $50,000 in the Diamond Match collapse the year before his death and frittered away $30,000 on horses and traps. Luckily there was some insurance.

Ketcham Will Case

Agreement Reached Between Toledo Relatives and the Widow
Oshkosh (WI) Daily Northwestern, Monday, January 24, 1898

A settlement of the Ketcham will case has been practically affected. It will never air in court. An agreement has been reached between the wife of John B. Ketcham, who lives in Chicago, and the two brothers, George H. and Valentine, and a sister, Mrs. Mary Nearing, living in Toledo. The terms of the agreement are private and George Ketcham today refused to discuss the subject beyond admitting a settlement. Friends of the family believe that Minnie Wallace Walkup Ketcham will receive about $73,000; Nettie Poe Ketchum [*sic*], the first wife, will receive $5000 in life insurance, the brothers and sisters will receive the remainder of the estate, bringing back to Toledo about $200,000. The total life insurance was $78,000.

But that wasn't all Minnie had gotten from Ketcham. He'd showered her with expensive gifts when he was absolutely infatuated with her. Once imprisoned by her, she'd collected his stocks and bonds and rummaged through his safe deposit boxes. Who knows what else she pilfered. She certainly ended up with enough money to live well until the next silly old man came along. And, of course, he did.

7

THE COMPANY SHE KEEPS

YOUNG, LOVELY, AND TWICE WIDOWED, MINNIE DIDN'T retire into a quiet life of good works in hopes of regaining her reputation—if she'd ever had much of one to begin with. Instead, she again gravitated to the demimonde, a lifestyle where beautiful women and wealthy men enjoyed the hedonistic pleasures of life. Here were nights dining at such elegant restaurants as De Jonghe's Hotel and Restaurant at 12 East Monroe Street, run by three Belgian brothers who are credited with creating "shrimp de Jonghe," a classic Chicago dish.

Late evenings might find this group at less fancy watering holes, such as Frank Wing's in Chicago's storied and sordid Levee district, known for offering all the vices humankind could want. It was the type of place where a waiter stabbing another to death warranted just a small paragraph in the papers.

Minnie's female friends were often called actresses, though most really were less inclined toward a career on the stage than in landing a moneyed man who'd pay for a lush apartment, showy jewelry, fine furnishings, furs, and clothes. If they were lucky, they might even inveigle an offer of marriage, though often there were serious impediments to that outcome—the besotted suitor might have the inconvenience of a wife and family. If he was single, horrified parents would do almost anything to break up the relationship.

These adventuresses were often like shooting stars. Discovered by a rich man or two or often even more, they were lavished with adoration, attention, gifts, and promises, but eventually most of them, looks and money gone, ended up forgotten and forlorn. These were compatriots of Minnie, women who were friends or at least contemporaries and so deserve their time here as well, since they offer a further look into the life she led as she made her way in Chicago.

Meteoric Careers in Chicago of Five New Orleans Beauties
(Chicago) Inter Ocean, Sunday, December 7, 1902

The reign of a quintet of New Orleans beauties has closed.

Of this quintet of youthful beauties that swooped down upon Chicago from New Orleans Josephine Moffit, who failed in the courts to prove that she was the common-law wife of William Wallace Pike, is the last to go. . . . Less than a decade ago when all who love the madding crowd were scurrying to the World's Fair city, these young women were the main event here. Their debut was marked by no clamor, but their subsequent careers had a lurid tinge of glory about them. They made much history for Chicago's giddy throng.

Most of the five lived in lavish splendor. Their gowns inspired wonder among the best dressed women in the United States. Their equipage was the handsomest that wealthy Chicago men could hire. Their throats blazed with jewels. Fortunes melted away at their smiles, with the inevitable result that of many well-known men, with the inevitable result that the names of many well-known men, both married and single, were carried over the city on the winds of gossip which was an akin to scandal.

These young women, most of whom knew each other in the Crescent city and came to Chicago together formed a most remarkable coterie. Most of them were in their teens but all were extremely beautiful and have caught a glimpse of the giddiest life in the southern metropolis.

Such was the gift of New Orleans to Chicago.

It sent to the world's fair a beauty show of its own. The fortunes that were wasted in lavish living, the priceless jewels that were showered upon the women, the deserted wives, and the crowded court rooms, find space in the story of most of these women. They were still comparatively young, but the eyes of the world are turned in other directions.

Beneath these words were photos of five women, Minnie Wallace Walkup Ketcham among them. The others were Zella Nicolaus, May Reed Pesia, Josephine Moffitt, and Minnie Copeland, known as Corinne Kimball. The last, the adopted daughter of actress and stage mother Jennie Kimball, actually earned fame for her acting, debuting at the age of two and a half and performing in a major production at age five.

Jennie Kimball lost custody of her daughter when taken to court in 1881 by the Society for the Prevention of Cruelty to Children, which argued that the eight-year-old Corinne didn't attend either school or church. The judge concurred, and Kimball temporarily lost custody. Another court hearing and a more liberal-leaning judge wrote in his decision that the US Constitution safeguarded Corinne's parents (he used the term *guardians*) from being punished for not taking her to church. Corinne returned to her home and the stage and seven years later had her own touring company known as both the Kimball Opera Company and the Corinne Opera Company.

In 1896, when she was twenty-two, the *New York Times* described her as a "goldmine" for her mother and "the most famous of all the child actresses of this country." She performed in burlesque shows covered in extravagant jewels that were said to be the real deal. Two years later, when her mother died of pneumonia in her private train car, she left Corinne an estate valued at $600,000 ($6,365,940 today), and Corinne, probably exhausted after more than two decades of touring—at age five, she played the role of Buttercup in *Pinafore* one hundred times—retired from the stage. In future years, she turned up occasionally in news accounts—for a broken engagement with a prince and that kind of thing. But all in all, it doesn't seem to have turned out badly for Corinne and her mother; though obviously guilty of not sending her to Sunday school, she managed Corinne's career and money quite well—ensuring her daughter had a cushy life.

Indiana to Paris and Back Again

Rosella Lytle grew up in a series of charming but small Indiana towns, the daughter of David Lytle. She was one among many children in a poor family. Moving from Wabash to the somewhat bigger city of Logansport at age fifteen, Rosella, soon to be known as Zella Nicolaus, ran off with traveling salesman Harvey Christmann. If it was a romance, it didn't last long, and she soon blackmailed him for a sum of $100 ($2,443)—a measly amount compared to what she would later try to extort from men who fell for her charms.

Relentlessly restless, the beautiful baby-faced blonde moved out west and by 1891 had landed in New Orleans. Before long, though, she headed north, scooping up a detective as she traveled through her home state. He set her up in a flat at 5206 Wabash Avenue in Chicago. She was still a teenager at the time and definitely on her way up in terms of men.

Soon the detective was replaced by a wealthy widower with children. She married him and moved to Joliet, Illinois, where he owned a dry goods store. He gave her whatever she wanted, but it wasn't enough, and Zella soon was back in Chicago, where she enraptured a city official who set her up in an Ohio Street apartment. When that fizzled, Zella moved to New York for a time and then back to Chicago, where she lived in the Great Northern Hotel in a suite of rooms costing fifty dollars a day.

Before long she'd settled in the Sturtevant House in New York, where her hotel bills for her six-week stay ranged from $250 to more than $300 (the latter is equal to about $7,000 today). A noted actor who asked to be anonymous when he was quoted for a *Chicago Tribune* article dated Thursday, December 7, 1893, gave her acting lessons.

Zella wanted to start her own stage company as quickly as possible, the anonymous actor said, adding that she told him money was not a problem. But money always is. Her source of cash ran out, and Zella was forced to check out of the hotel, leaving four of her trunks as collateral for her unpaid bills. When asked by the cashier of the hotel what the matter was, she replied a friend had failed to keep a promise.

Zella was eighteen when she somehow came into possession of a check for $40,000 (about $1,081,319 today). Speculation was that she procured it from Howard Gould, of the wealthy New York Gould family. We can most likely count Zella as one of the reasons Howard's wife would later sue him because of his flagrant infidelity. Unable to cash it, Zella began negotiations with another family member, George Gould, described as a calculating businessman and most likely much more levelheaded than Howard when it came to women.

Gould, feeling sorry for her (or at least that's what he told reporters), gave her money to return to Chicago. But, of course, Zella didn't stay there.

"Within a week she returned to my office again and said her departure for Chicago had been delayed and confessed she had been obliged to spend part of the money which I had given her and therefore did not have enough to enable her to return home," he said in December 1893. "Therefore, I gave her some more money but when she came back again a week later I refused to see her because I had then decided that she was not telling the truth. That is all I know about the woman."

Not one to give up easily, Zella continued harassing the family. George Gould's employees told how she'd camp out in his office for hours, refusing to believe them when they told her he wasn't there. This went on for a year. She also asserted that Gould had assaulted her and asked for another $50,000 as compensation. Finally, two years later, the Goulds caved.

A. L. Ruhman, husband of Zella Nicolaus, assured a reporter today that his wife had settled her case with George Gould, in which a $40,000 check was involved.

"You can say that the suit against George Gould brought by my wife has been settled, and that all legal proceedings have been discontinued. I prefer that Mrs. Ruhman tell the terms of the settlement herself. We leave here for Chicago on Monday. It is Mrs. Ruhman's intention to return to the stage."

The report is current in Jersey City, where the Ruhmans' counsel reside, that the amount paid by Mr. Gould was not more than $5000 [$135,164.95 in today's money] of which sum Mrs. Ruhman received $1000, her husband $1000 and the counsel $1000, the balance going to pay the costs of litigation.

A later story said that Zella took her share of the cash and departed for Paris, where she lived lavishly until she spent it all. Broke, she and Ruhman were back in Chicago, where he was arrested for vagrancy. She was twenty-two at the time—they'd gone through the money very quickly—and already her looks were said to be fading. Her acting career was a failure, and in 1899, she announced she was returning to Wabash to live a quiet life.

Within a decade she would be dead. Country life obviously wasn't healthy for her.

Baby Jo

Josephine Moffitt, like Minnie, hailed from New Orleans, where she was known as Josephine Guillmette (also spelled Guillemet), and there's a likely chance they knew each other, at least in passing. They were born just four days apart—Josephine on January 10, 1869, and Minnie on January 14—and both attended Ursuline Academy, a well-respected convent school. The two also were similar in that their religious education had little effect on their moral behavior.

In Chicago, Minnie and Josephine both lived at 1401 Michigan Avenue, but they arrived under very different conditions.

Minnie's parents divorced; Josephine's parents had never married. Indeed, her father, the French-born Adrien Guillemet, already had a wife and family, though that didn't stop him from begetting eight children with Josephine's mother, his common-law wife, a mulatto woman named Josephine Carrel Carleton. Her mother's racial heritage meant that Josephine was also considered a person of color, but once she left New Orleans, she hid her heritage and always passed for white.

Though Josephine would later tell a jury she was nine when her father died of smallpox in 1884, she was actually fifteen. But that was Josephine; when she was forty, she passed herself off as twenty. A courtesan's shelf life was short, and the men who supported them liked their women young; call it a necessary business decision to lie about her age. (For a quick reference of that truism, we direct you to Minnie's life story.)

By the time her father died, Josephine was no longer attending the convent school and had moved to a neighborhood near the St. Charles hotel, where prosperous planters frequently stayed—another good business decision on her part. She quickly caught the eye of a wealthy traveler from Baton Rouge. Her charms were such that a rivalry between the capitalist and another man led to a shooting in front of the Henry Clay monument. Knowledgeable about common-law marriages, she tried to inveigle into one with the man from Baton Rouge, but he must have had other plans. Before she could file a law suit, two men threatened to tar and feather her unless she left New Orleans.

Luckily, that move was easily facilitated when J. Westley Moffitt, a married man, abandoned his wife and children to run off with Josephine. In court, she described him as her guardian, but we don't believe it.

Mrs. Moffitt followed the couple to Hot Springs, Arkansas, where her husband was managing a hotel owned by his brother-in-law. She begged her husband to return, but Moffitt, who was in his late twenties, wasn't interested in his wife and children and stayed with the beautiful teenager in the appropriately named Hot Springs.

Even the truest of loves doesn't last, and Moffitt, obviously not the faithful type, absconded without Josephine and headed to Chicago. But like Mrs. Moffitt, Josephine, showing a tenacity that she would use with the many runaway men in her future, wasn't about to let him go that easily. Leaving Hot Springs, she also left behind her last name and entered Chicago, where Moffitt was staying, with the new title of Mrs. Moffitt. The original owner of that name was staying at the Maine Hotel, and because they both liked to drink in excess, there was some heavy-duty partying. But alas, this Mr. and Mrs. Moffitt weren't meant to be any more than the previous Moffits were. Besides, by now Moffitt was deep in debt.

Thus the reunion was short-lived, and before long, Josephine was sharing an apartment with Gladys Forbes, who ran the Monroe restaurant. Gladys matched up pretty young women and wealthy men. One night, when a group of young well-to-do men who came from wealthy families entered the Monroe House for a night of celebrating the impending marriage of Gale Thompson, the scion of one of Chicago's most respected and wealthy families, Gladys invited her young beauties to come over and meet the boys. Josephine's next adventure was about to start.

Among the men was William Pike, a young bachelor who lived with his parents in the family's palatial home. Somewhat overweight as well as a lightweight, Billie (as he was called) was seemingly unambitious, spending his time spending his family's vast amounts of money. Also among the group was Gale's brother, the colorful and outspoken William Hale Thompson, a rising Republican political star who instead of going to Yale University, as his family expected, moved to Wyoming at age fourteen, becoming a cowboy and cattle rancher. Thompson, who returned to Chicago after his father's death in 1899 to take over management of the family's vast real estate holdings, would later testify that Josephine met William Pike at Frank Wing's, where the two went after leaving the Monroe House, and the two later lived together at 2342 Calumet Avenue. Josephine quibbled about where they met, saying it was at the Monroe but that they ended up at Wing's. They also disagreed about other events that evening. Thompson said he heard Josephine invite Pike home following a lot of kissing and fondling at Wing's. It wasn't like that at all, said Josephine. Poor Billie was sick, and so she invited him home to take care of him.

Dear reader, which story do you believe?

Billie Pike was, in turns, infatuated, manipulated, and bullied by Josephine in a tumultuous relationship that lasted several years. When he tried to break it off, once even asking his lawyer to do it, she seduced him back into the relationship or tormented him by standing outside of the large home where he lived with his family. Indeed, during the trial that ensued, Pike's lawyers also brought up an incident in which Josephine, dressed very flamboyantly (read slutty), sat on the stoop of the family's home and loudly engaged in conversation with a passerby. She also wrote them letters. All this in hopes they'd pay her to go away.

Others were writing letters as well, keeping the Pikes informed about their son's behavior. One such missive, published in the *Inter Ocean* on November 30, 1902, read: "Mr. Pike—You had better look after your son Billy. He is keeping a woman in an apartment who is the daughter of a negress in New Orleans. She is trying her best to get Billy to marry her. In a recent trial in this city, which was settled quickly, this fact would have been brought out if the trial had been allowed to go on and would have caused a scandal. You had better watch Bill and find out."

Another anonymous letter reiterated Josephine's African American heritage. Back then, particularly in the South, being even an eighth black, or what was called an "octaroon," led to social ostracism from white society—even though by the logic of the time one-eighth black was more white than not. Didn't matter. Racism overrode logic, and of course, the ultimate logic is that all people are created equal.

Josephine hadn't confided her secret to many—maybe Minnie and Gladys, as they were all friends. Who then had written the letter to the Pikes? We're guessing Gladys; after all, she would go on to testify against Josephine during the trial, and she also testified against Minnie when she went to court again a few years later. But Josephine believed it was Minnie's lawyer, Dethlef Hansen, angry because she turned against Minnie in the Walkup case. Of course, Dethlef sued Minnie, too. It was, indeed, a group of vipers.

We are going to digress here to talk about Gladys. Her history remains elusive, but she appears to have been heartless and greedy—two good characteristics for her line of work.

Sometime in the summer of 1897, she met Homer B. Hitt, the son of a state senator and a young widower whose wife, Mrs. Lucy W. Treat of Polo, Illinois, had died giving birth to their child. Lucy, as the saying goes, was barely cold in her grave when Homer hit the big city of Chicago with his wife's inheritance—$60,000 left in trust with him for the baby. Gladys knew a sucker when she saw one and immediately married Homer. Within nine months, that $60,000 was down to $15,000, and the newlyweds were in court, charged with squandering the money. The remainders of poor Lucy's inheritance were taken away from the Hitts and given to the step-grandmother of the child, by then eleven months old. What happened to the baby after that, we don't know, but we hope her later life went better than that first year.

We are sad to report that the marriage of Gladys and Homer didn't weather the court proceedings and his losing all that lovely money.

Gladys was never one to stay out of the papers, and before long she was in the news again.

Woman Intruder Set Free
Gladys Forbes, Accused of Breaking Furniture in
Huron Street Residence, Not Prosecuted.
Chicago Tribune, Saturday, August 27, 1904

After attacking a Chinese butler, smashing a mirror, it is charged, and doing other damage at the residence of William Hulin, 334 Huron Street, Gladys Forbes was set free yesterday. When the case was called in the East Chicago Avenue police court neither

Toy Gett, the servant, nor Mr. Hulin was present to prosecute. The policeman who had made the arrest also had lost interest over night.

Miss Forbes, who she lived at 2229 Wabash Avenue, declared she had gone to the Huron Street residence in response to a telephone message. When she tried to enter she says the servant stopped her and the trouble resulted. Toy Gett told the police when they reached the house in response to his appeal for help that the young woman had beaten him. He said she had a made a mistake in the telephone address.

The story becomes even more intriguing upon learning that Mr. Hulin was a well-to-do and seemingly respectable citizen who was a member of the Hall & Ross Husking Glove Company and secretary of the Chicago Wood Finishing Company. With a Chinese butler, or really any type of butler, he was clearly among the aristocracy of Chicago, so one has to wonder what Gladys was up to and why neither Toy Gett, nor the arresting policeman, nor Mr. Hulin showed up in court. Did Gladys's shady connections get to them?

Before long, Gladys claimed to be married again, though the two hadn't actually gone through a ceremony, and was calling herself Gladys Shannon. She and her husband (we'll call him that because she did), Thomas Shannon, had somehow acquired a little girl and were seeking to adopt her. Yes, I know what you're thinking—Gladys, a mother? But maybe there was a deep maternal instinct in Gladys struggling to get out or maybe there were more nefarious reasons one doesn't want to consider. Anyway, if you're thinking Gladys would be an awful mother to ten-year-old Margaret Thorpe, so did the Catholic Sisters at the Foundling House, who after investigating Gladys and Tom, decided that the Shannons weren't the best prospects for parenthood.

Acting on the judge's order, an attorney tried to take little Margaret back to the Foundling House. But we think Margaret had already stayed too long with the Shannons. Asking to use the restroom, Margaret made her escape and was joined by the Shannons. When authorities went to investigate, they found only bare walls and floors in an apartment that had been handsomely decorated a few hours earlier. All the furniture, as well as Gladys, Thomas, and Margaret, was gone.

One would hope that having a loving kidnapping mother like Gladys would have made this young girl grow up into a solid citizen. But, as you, dear readers, might guess, that wasn't to be. In 1924, Margaret Forbes was arrested for horsewhipping a person.

These types of murky messes were commonplace occurrences for Minnie and her friends.

Now let's get back to poor Josephine. Billie had long known she was a wanton woman and still had loved and supported her. But being a Negro? That was too much.

He was totally done with her, but if he thought it was going to be that easy, he didn't know his Josephine, who definitely wasn't finished with him. Josephine filed a suit of separate maintenance on the grounds that he, her lawful husband, had deserted her and refused to support her. To get rid of Moffitt, the Pike family reportedly offered an annuity of $2,500 for five years, which totals in today's money to about $337,912. All she had to do was return all the letters Billie had written to her and leave Chicago. Josephine countered, asking for $60,000 ($1,621,979.43) a year. She would have done better to take the money and move on because the Pikes decided to fight her in court. Billie, by now willing to listen completely to his parents and being well schooled by his lawyers, said their relationship was "professional" because of her status as a courtesan.

The ensuing court battle was brutal both in and out of court.

Child of Ketcham Case
(Chicago) *Inter Ocean*, Friday, November 21, 1902

Former Judge John Barton Payne, one of Pike's attorneys, scoffed at the idea that Billie and Josephine were in anyway joined legally given her status in life and her past.

"It is impossible that a woman like this could conceive the meaning of the matrimonial service, of those holy bonds into which she says she entered," he orated. "Why, if it pleased your honor, this is but a child of the Ketcham case—a child reared under the direction of that woman whom death aided in an infamous pursuit of wealth."

Big Bill Thompson testified that Josephine's behavior "disgusted" him. The other women making up the female portion of group included Freckled Sal, Sheeney Coral, and Baby Jo (which also was one of Josephine's nicknames, but I guess there were two with the same moniker). One has to wonder why, if women like these were so abhorrent to Thompson, he even joined the party. Could it really be true, as he told the court, that he didn't know them very well at all? And couldn't he, smart guy that he was, have figured out what type of ladies they were?

After recounting his story to the jury, Thompson beat it out of town—thinking his career possibly over, but upon his return, he found his political rise unimpeded. He went on to become elected mayor of Chicago three times, serving from 1915 to 1923 and again from 1927 to 1931. Over six feet tall and weighing in at more than three hundred pounds helped earned him the nickname "Big Bill," but his outrageous personality also contributed to that moniker.

Thanks to his days as a cattle rancher, he thought of himself as a cowboy, once riding a horse into the city council chamber. A champion of civil rights, he was also extremely corrupt, and scandals kept him from running for a third term in 1923, allowing reformer William Dever to step in as mayor. In his anti-corruption zeal, Dever closed speakeasies and drove mobster Al Capone out of town; Capone then set up headquarters in nearby Cicero. Chicagoans didn't mind a little reform, but they still needed a place to drink. Seizing on that, when Thompson ran against Dever in 1927, he told voters, "When I'm elected we will not only re-open places these people closed but we'll open 10,000 new ones. . . . No copper will invade your home and fan your mattress for a hip flask."

Capone played his civic part in assisting Thompson in his reelection campaign, contributing an estimated quarter of a million dollars to the cause. The cozy relationship between Big Bill and Al is one reason why a 1993 panel of well-respect historians named Thompson the worst mayor in American history. Whether that honor still holds, we're not sure since there have been a lot of recent competitors in the contest. But Thompson left another lasting mark on Chicago politics—he was its last Republican mayor.

When his man won, Capone was so delighted that he hung a portrait of Big Bill in his headquarters. Thompson returned the favor, appointing Capone compatriot Daniel Serritella as city sealer. This position allowed a direct line of communication between Capone and city hall. Capone felt so emboldened that he not only expanded his Hotel Metropole headquarters in the city but also set up a gambling operation just a block away from city hall. After all, why should city hall cronies have to walk any farther than that to place a bet—and toss back a drink or two?

As for Thompson, as the story goes, he celebrated aboard the Fish Fans Boat Club in Belmont Harbor, which federal agents believed to a be a floating speakeasy. Not so, said Thompson; it was just a place for fisherman to relax. The weight of all the revelers aboard that boat caused the boat to sink into the mud, dispensing so many gallons of gin into the harbor that jokers called it the largest martini in the world.

Thompson lost his next election to another reformer, Anton Cermak, who made Big Bill's cozy relationship with Capone the central plank of the campaign. Thompson mocked Cermak, a Bohemian immigrant, calling him "Pushcart Tony." But Chicago was a city of immigrants, and ethnic voters didn't take to that.

"He doesn't like my name," Cermak retorted. "It's true I didn't come over on the *Mayflower*, but I came over as soon as I could."

Poor Cermak wouldn't make it through his first term. In Miami, he was invited by Franklyn D. Roosevelt to sit with him on top of the back seat of a convertible. The two were shaking hands when Giuseppe Zangara raised a hand gun and fired, intent on killing Roosevelt. He was a very bad shot, hitting Cermak and four others. Mortally wounded, Cermak, always good with a line (see above his retort to Thompson), said to Roosevelt, "I am glad it was me instead of you."

When Thompson, credited as the creator of Chicago-style twentieth-century politics and the image of a politician on the take, died in 1944, he left an estate estimated at $2 million. Another $1.84 million in cash was discovered in two safe deposit boxes in his name. Don't you just love Chicago politics?

There is nothing to indicate that Minnie ever had a relationship with Big Bill, who married, against his mother's wishes, Mary "Maysie" Walker, a secretary in the family business. But he certainly at times intersected with her social group, as did his two brothers, Gale and Percy. Like Minnie, Big Bill straddled two societies—the well-connected and well-to-do and those who were part of Chicago's storied Levee.

The case was wonderfully scandalous, and citizens of Chicago and beyond couldn't get enough.

"More wine, more women and more song, together with more cabs, more automobiles, more midnight adventures and more of everything, in fact that made life worth the living to William Wallace Pike while he and the woman now suing for recognition as his wife, were spending their hours together, were introduced in the hearing of the case yesterday," reported the *Inter Ocean* on November 18, 1902.

A Nest of Vipers

Josephine's case against Pike wasn't helped any by her once great friend Gladys Forbes.

"Baby Jo" Broiled by a New Witness
Former Friend Relates More Features of Pike Scandal
Wine and Embraces
Court Hears of Champagne, Kisses, and Late Cab Rides
(*Chicago*) *Inter Ocean*, Tuesday, November 18, 1902

Mrs. Hite-Shannon-Forbes Takes Stand—Watchman
Tells of Anxiety for "Donkey-Boy Billie."

Gladys had entered the court earlier that afternoon gorgeously gowned and wearing a heavy veil.

"My name?" she repeated in a languid voice as she raised a bouquet of violets to her face.

Ex-judge Payne asked if she were married, and Gladys acknowledged she had been but that there had been a divorce.

While she talked, she tapped the railing nervously with her gray gloves.

She had met Josephine in 1896, when the young woman had arrived with letters of introduction from a Mrs. Hankins, wife of a well-known gambler. Josephine first acted as a maid for Gladys and then became her companion. Even after Josephine moved on, she and Gladys remained good friends—that is, until Gladys had some trouble because a dozen cream puffs and an angel food cake were charged to the Moffitt-Pike account in the bakery beneath the Follansbee flat. With all the money floating around, it seems difficult to believe these two great friends—Gladys and Josephine—would fall out over cream puffs and cakes. It makes one wonder if they really were so petty, if there were other issues too, or if Josephine, who was sensually plump, ordered way too many expensive pastries.

Before they morphed into enemies, Gladys remembered a certain supper-ceremony between "Sugar Heart Josie" and "Donkey Boy Bill" in the Masonic temple restaurant. Josie was plotting to capture Billie or persuade his family to give up some of their millions.

The two women would drive by Billie's house after he and Josie had broken up. Gladys asked if she wanted Billie to come up and see her, to which Josie replied that she didn't want to see him, that all she was after was his money. If she could get reporters to go to the home where Billie lived with his mother, she thought the family would pay her off.

Josephine's lawyers tried hitting Gladys hard—impugning her morals and lifestyle.

"Who was your husband at the time, Madame?" asked Mr. Bishop after Gladys had indignantly declared she was a respectable married woman (we didn't hear if the courtroom broke out in laughter).

"Why it was—let me see—why, Mr. Hitt, of course."

"Are you positive, Madame?"

"Well, this was in—oh yes, I'm sure about it."

Poor Josephine, up until then the papers had been predicting she'd win her suit. The pile on continued with Pike's lawyer also disparaging Josephine's past, bringing up her relationship with Mr. Moffitt. She, in turn, still insisted he'd been her guardian.

"Do you know where your guardian's wife was at this time?" the attorney asked and then answered his own question. "She was at Carbondale, wasn't she? A brokenhearted woman on account of your having run away with her husband."

Josephine's attorney objected, saying, "I don't think that is proper."

The End of Billie and Josephine

Josephine lost her case, with the judge deciding she wasn't Pike's common-law wife and stating, "Mrs. Moffitt's morality is on par with that of the defendant."

Gifford was possibly won over by Pike's attorney, who expressed doubts that William Wallace Pike, who loved his mother as he did, could fall in love with a woman like Josephine. He also showed, without meaning to, the state of his own marriage, saying that husbands and wives didn't drown themselves in kisses the way that Josephine and Billie had:

> They kiss perhaps when he goes away to do business in the morning—at least they used to but I understand that custom has gone out of vogue. These kisses spoken of in the testimony were not those of married persons. She pressed her large and luscious lips upon the equally large and luscious lips of my client, and then he would go downtown and sign a lease or write a foolish letter.
>
> Willie may have been proprietor of a pair of ears which overshadowed his intellect, but not to one of those letters did he sign himself "husband." Nor did he, in any of them, call her "wife."

Maintaining that Josephine was a schemer, Pike's attorney then brought up Gladys Forbes, asking how the plaintiff's lawyers could criticize her by saying she was that type of woman, noting Josephine had been her friend for years.

"The complainant went with Gladys Forbes to many places which she admits were of ill repute," he argued to the judge, implying that by sullying Gladys's reputation, they were surely disparaging Josephine as well.

What does that say about Minnie? She, Gladys, and Josephine seldom lived farther from each other than a few blocks in all the years Minnie spent in Chicago.

Josephine wasn't a quitter, and after losing the trial, she filed an appeal. The Pike family was said to have offered her a large sum of money. She denied accepting it, but we don't believe that.

Josephine's drama wasn't just a harbinger of Minnie's past but also of her imminent future. Several of the players appearing in court, including Billie's lawyer, would appear again the following year when Minnie once more found herself in court, this time defending herself in response to a lawsuit from Dethlef Hansen, the attorney who helped her secure a chunk of Ketcham's fortune. Minnie and her friends kept the courtrooms, attorneys, and newspapers very busy indeed, and as a journalist, I want to thank her.

Leaving Chicago, Josephine traveled to New York. But her intent wasn't to become a show girl, not after the chance of becoming a princess presented itself in the Big Apple.

8

MOVING ON UP

In Which Josephine Captures and Loses a Prince

GOING ON STAGE (READ CHORUS LINE) IN NEW YORK IN THE show *The Great White Way*, Josephine caught the eye of Prince Victor Theodore Maximilian Egon Maria Lamoral von Thurn and Taxis, a member of one of the oldest families in all Europe and a seemingly big fish who came to New York in 1906.

Billie Pike looked like a—excuse our pun—piker compared to this nobleman who proposed marriage to her almost immediately (as Josephine tells it), though he also explained—and it would turn out he had tried this trick before—they couldn't marry in a church until certain obstacles were removed. Nevertheless, they clasped hands across the table where they were sitting drinking cocktails and pledged themselves to each other. Unfortunately, the marriage was doomed. Having bedded Josephine, the prince's ardor quickly cooled, and he disappeared, catching a ship back to Europe.

Who was Prince Victor? The short answer is he was a cad, swindler, and poverty-stricken aristocrat who came from an ancient noble family. Despite his title, the prince had little money of his own and was actually in New York to snare a rich wife—on someone else's dime. Even Josephine, who swore she was married to him, knew he was trying to snag a well-to-do woman. He hadn't been able to get a New York heiress but had hopes for a southern lady worth $2 million and said to be a Vanderbilt. Princess Josephine, as she liked to call herself after their six-week affair, had written to his brother Maximillian in Vienna about this $2 million prospect—maybe to try to sour the affair.

Maximillian was not impressed with the amount and immediately sent Victor a cablegram reading, "Do not disgrace yourself by marrying a girl who is worth only $2 million. You must get a wife worth at least $20 million."

Prince Victor was in a big mess. The fashionable set were rejecting him because of all the scandals, creditors were hounding him day and night, his "table d'hote bride" (as one news wag described Josephine) was asking where the money was to come from to pay their huge expenses, as they lived like king and queen—or at least, prince and princess.

> There was just one thing to do—and the noble Prince did it, in terms of American slang he "beat it. . ." without sending a memorandum of his address in Europe to his creditors, and without even a farewell understanding with his table d'hote bride, this noble Prince of the great house of Thurn and Taxis hopped on a steamer and disappeared.
>
> —*Pittsburgh Press* in a Sunday, December 11, 1921

As soon as news reached that the prince had sailed away, creditors swooped down on his Park Avenue apartment, which had been his love nest with Princess Josephine. Moving vans backed up and took away the furniture, which, of course, had been purchased on credit. Jewelers' clerks ransacked the place and took away any valuables they could find. An artist sent over a man to recover a portrait of the prince he'd painted after being promised that it would be put on exhibition in the Thurn and Taxis palace.

Never one to be deterred and desperately wanting to keep her princess title—besides, the apartment was now bare—Josephine once again pursued a male who deserted her, selling her jewels to book passage across the Atlantic Ocean.

"He would never have left me as he had of his own free will," she said about the runaway prince. "His family, I believe, found that I had no money and they were angry with him for marrying me."

She wasn't the only one chasing after the beleaguered royal.

Prince Victor Is in More Trouble
Costly Wardrobe Seized by Court to Secure Heavy Debts
Paris News and Comment
Paul Villiers Relates Latest Happenings in French Capital.
Salt Lake Herald Republican, Sunday, May 17, 1908

Prince Victor of Thurn and Taxis seems to be prosecuted by a nemesis which follows him everywhere. Having just escaped from the London courts, where he had to appear to defend himself in an action brought against him by Mrs. Josephine Moffitt, an American girl who claims he married and deserted her, he came to Paris only to find himself in an even worse plight, for now he has nothing left but the clothes on his back.

The Prince's whole wardrobe and all his personal belongings have been seized by the police on the complaint of Mademoiselle Wilhelmina Kemper, who declares she is going to sell them at public auction unless Prince Victor settles with her.

The complainant had a fortune of $150,000 and having made the acquaintance of the Comtesse de Clare and Count Zoltinsky, was persuaded by them to advance money to Prince Victor in order that he might be enabled to contract a wealthy marriageable woman.

Mlle. Kemper declares she advanced $150,000 whilst according to the Prince, it only amounted to $44,000.

Mlle. Kemper, who is a middle-aged woman, found the prince was in Paris and staying at the Hotel de France et de Choisel. She promptly went to her lawyer and instructed him to levy distraint [the seizure of someone's property in order to obtain payment of money owed] on the clothing and personal belongings of the prince. A bailiff went to the room occupied by the Prince and levied a distraint on prince's valise and all the clothes he was not standing up in.

The prince was exceedingly annoyed at this preceding. He found it extremely awkward to be deprived of his wardrobe.

However an arrangement was come to. The bailiff took an inventory of all the prince's belongings and then offered to make the prince the man in possession of his own clothes. This is a custom in the case of the distraints in France.

The prince accordingly accepted the responsibility of being placed in charge as a legal custodian of his own clothes. But he cannot remove the clothes from the hotel unless the distraint is removed and Mlle. Kemper refuses to remove it.

In an interview, Mlle. Kemper said: "I seized the prince's belongings because he is a foreigner with no resident of his own in France, affects constitute my only security. I advanced the money to the prince to enable him to contract a wealthy marriage with an American heiress, understood to be Miss Vanderbilt."

The clothing held for ransom (so to speak) bespoke the Prince's lack of funds. His three suits of clothes were described as much worn. He also had two dinner jackets, two evening suits, three canes, 26 handkerchiefs, sundry toilet articles, four suits of underclothes, two overcoats, three canes—one with a golden head with the prince's arms engraved on it, a silver cigarette case and four scarf pins, one with an imitation pearl on it.

The prince was a very bad investment indeed.

Speculation in Prince Proved to be Disastrous
Woman Risked All to Forward Cause of Alleged Royalty
He Was to Marry Wealthy Helpmeet
Two Companions Persuaded Her to Part with About $120,000
Asheville Citizen-Times, Sunday, July 21, 1912

Miss Wilhelmina Kemper, who is of German origin, as her name indicates, but has been naturalized in France, began an action some four years ago against an Englishwoman who calls herself the Countess of Clare, the widow of Sir Herbert Crosley, and against a Pole, Count Ladislas Michel de Zoltinsky [sometimes spelled Zoltynsky], accusing them of having swindled her of $120,000. A decision has just been rendered which will be final and unless an appeal is taken to Court.

The business which brought these three people together in the first place was to provide a certain Prince Victor Theodor Maximilian Egon Maria Lamoral von Thurn and Taxis, or one who so styles himself, with a wife. The Prince describes himself as a nephew of the Emperor of Austria. The English countess and the Polish count as friends of the Prince succeeded in interesting Miss Kemper in him. This decision just given says:

"Miss Kemper was introduced by the widow Crossley in October 1905, by one Geiger, who the widow Crossley represented to be her secretary or man of business but who later appeared in the light of a beater up of questionable affairs. On November 12, 1905, two agreements by private deed drawn up by Geiger were signed, by which Ms. Kemper and the widow Crossley each undertook to advance to Prince Victor of Thurn and Taxis a loan of $10,000 at the rate of 5%."

This first advance evidently proved insufficient for its object, as a fortnight later Ms. Kemper provided $96,000 more and three months later, in February 1906, $20,273.80. The Prince, however, was still not provided with a helpmeet. The Countess of Claire and Count Zoltinsky about this time informed Ms. Kemper that the Prince was probably about to marry an American millionaire's daughter. Such a marriage, they pointed out to her, could not be carried out without some expense and Miss Kemper—in the hope no doubt in being repaid in American gold—making a total sum of nearly $120,000. Not to allow Ms. Kemper to rely merely on the hopes of American gold, Count Zoltinsky gave her for security 7/17th in a manganese mine concession which he possessed in Ivanofska, Russia.

Now penniless, Miss Kemper awaited the return of her money with interest in vain. She began to doubt the wisdom of her investment and questioned the good faith of the English countess and the Polish count, and her doubts turned to conviction. In February 1910, she brought the case before the Correctional Court. When the case was heard, some edifying details were given on the past life of Count Zoltinsky and witnesses came forward to identify the Countess of Clare as a certain Blanche Leigh, once a perfume seller in the Rue de la Paix.

The Countess protested against these statements and brought witnesses to testify to her integrity and of that of Count Zoltinsky and in April the two were acquitted. But Miss Kemper was not satisfied at this end of her investment. She took the case to the Correctional Appeal Court, where it occupied three hearings and a fortnight deliberation before judgment was given.

As may be gathered from the questions already given from this judgment, it upset the lower court's verdict of acquittal and condemned Zoltinsky to two years in prison, with the fine of $400, and the widow Crossley—a Republican tribunal disdains to recognize titles—to one year in prison and a fine of $200. It requires Zoltinsky to refund to Mrs. Kemper all the money she advanced but considering that the widow Crossley's cooperation with Zoltinsky had only been established with respect to money advanced up to February 1906, the court ordered the two jointly and severally to re-pay this amount, $39,472. It also condemns them to pay $6,000 damages and with the thoroughness that always mark a French sentence it granted "constraint of body" which means that if the money is not paid the complainant can have them arrested and imprisoned. The findings which precede the sentences in the judgment shows that Zoltinsky, the widow Crossley and Geiger had conspired to find a wife for the Prince in return for a 5% commission on the marriage dowry.

Poor Josephine. If a Vanderbilt heiress worth $2 million wasn't good enough for the prince and his family, this New Orleans–bred chorus girl certainly wasn't going to make the grade. And Prince Victor, now that he'd seduced her (if one could really seduce the predatory Josephine), was done with the relationship.

If Victor missed out on Gladys Moore Vanderbilt, Count László Széchenyi of Hungary scooped her up. Unfortunately, though the couple had five daughters, Széchenyi was a compulsive gambler, which is how he lost his fortune. But Countess Széchenyi, née Gladys Vanderbilt, seems to have held on to much of the $25 million she inherited from her parents and showing more than a touch of class, during World War I, put her palace in Budapest at the disposal of the army for some six hundred reservists to be quartered there. She also used the palace as a hospital. She returned to Newport, Rhode Island, after inheriting the Breakers, a seventy-room Italian Renaissance–style palazzo inspired by the sixteenth-century palaces of Genoa and Turin and considered the most magnificent of those oceanfront "summer cottages" where the rich came to get away from it all during the Gilded Age. An ardent historic preservationist, Gladys opened the house for tours to raise money for the Preservation Society of Newport County and lived on the top floor. It now is a national historic landmark.

As for the countess really being a shop girl, why that wasn't true, testified the widow Crossley, though she also acknowledged that Blanche Leigh looked very much like her. And would you be surprised to find the shares of the manganese mine in Russia the monocle-wearing Count Zoltinsky had given Miss Kemper didn't exist at all? We thought not.

It was a trend back at the turn of the last century for rich American girls to marry penniless but titled European men. Anna Gould, who had also been on Prince Victor's list and worth $15 million, married another wastrel count over her family's vociferous objections. Her beloved was Paul Ernest Boniface de Castellane. She married him and became the countess de Castellane, as well as $5 to $10 million poorer (depending on news accounts).

> Nature gives to some men at their birth a love for music, painting, and sculpture; to Boni de Castellane she gave also a passion for women, horses, equipages, palaces, antiquities, and he got them all, wholesale. As a young man in Paris, Boni lived as a gay gallant and early complained that his parents did not give him sufficient spending money. The prodigal ran so deeply in debt that it is said his creditors, as a last resort, put him on a boat bound for America with instructions to marry an heiress.
>
> It was not Boni's idea to marry ever, but anything was better than poverty, and the penniless Comte Boni did as he was told with such speed and efficiency that his creditors were delighted. He was hardly landed in New York before he met and fascinated the most conspicuous heiress in sight, old Jay Gould's daughter, Anna. To Anna it was stepping into fairyland. To Boni it was just business, a bit of salesmanship and acting in order to raise a lot of money.
>
> "I came, I saw, I conquered," said Caesar, and Boni's famous description of how he conquered the "Golden Gould Girl," was almost as terse. He said:
>
> "Our eyes met, our hands met, our lips met and then our lawyers met."
>
> After the lawyers, it was said, had fixed up the deal so that the bride of the needy Comte would help him out of his debts and give him a million or so pocket money, they were married in the Gould mansion, March 4, 1895, the most important social event in many a year. While all the world was reading of his noble titles and ancestors and her millions and trousseau, the bridal couple embarked for Europe.
>
> —*Esoteric Curiosa* blog

The couple had five children before Anna divorced him. Two years after the divorce, she married Hélie de Talleyrand-Périgord and had two more children. He became a duke, making her a duchess. That marriage last until his death in 1937.

While his compatriots were wooing and wedding these fantastically rich heiresses, poor Prince Victor was trying to keep out of Josephine's clutches.

Prince Denies Wedding
Víctor of Thurn and Taxis Says He's Not Husband of Miss Moffitt.
New York Times, Sunday, March 22, 1908

Prince Victor of Thurn and Taxis told the Times correspondent today that the story of his marriage to a New York chorus girl named Moffitt was absolutely false.

"This statement of Josephine Moffitt that she was married to my brother sounds strange to me and I don't believe a word of it," said Prince Max of Thurn and Taxis when The New York Times correspondent met him emerging from the theater tonight. "Prince Victor is the sort of man who would let his family know if he married and knowing him as I do, I can't conceive of his having married Miss Moffitt, however estimable a young lady she may be."

The young woman who asserts that Prince Victor Thurn and Taxis married her left for Europe last Thursday, saying she was going to hunt for her husband. She declared just before sailing that she would even present her claims before the Austrian Emperor if Prince Victor did not acknowledge and take care of her.

The prince was not pleased. Deeply in debt, he didn't need an actress/courtesan claiming to be his wife—not if he was to catch rich bride, a necessary task if he wanted to keep living the high life. Toward the end of 1908, he filed suit in chancery court to keep Josephine from using his name, but Judge Sir Arthur Rolls Warrington was not as easy on him as the Chicago judge had been in letting Billie Pike off the hook. Motion denied. Josephine continued to call herself princess of Thurn and Taxis.

She soon, though, was going to be confronted with a woman who was even more tenacious than she.

Enter Lida Eleanor Nichols (Nicolls)

Born in 1875 in Uniontown, Pennsylvania, Lida was the daughter of a grocer, but more importantly, in terms of financial and social standing, she was the niece of Josiah B. Thompson, a Pittsburgh banker and coal and fuel operator. Her photos show an exceptionally lovely, poised, and aristocratic-looking woman.

Her first husband had the romantic and dashingly named General Gerald Purcell Fitzgerald. Described as "a Gentleman of The Island, County Waterford," he also was the nephew of Edward Fitzgerald, the poet who translated Omar Khayyam's "Rubaiyat of Omar Khayyam" from the original Persian into English. Fitzgerald came to Fayette County, Pennsylvania, to make money in the area's booming coal industry, the same field Lida's uncle excelled in. The two met, and shortly afterward, somewhat impetuously and most likely necessarily, they married on March 1, 1899, in Uniontown. Their son John Purcell Fitzgerald was born on September 24, 1899. History doesn't say whether he was born exceptionally premature. Two twins followed on October 25, 1900—Gerald Purcell Fitzgerald Jr. and Edward Maurice Purcell Fitzgerald.

Marry in haste, repent at leisure was not for Lida. By December 5, 1906, she had won her freedom from Fitzgerald but not before filing a petition in which she claimed her husband had dragged her from bed while she screamed and also at one point shook her so violently that her hat fell from her head and her hair came cascading down. Oh, my. But getting a divorce in the Irish courts wasn't easy at all. Parliament had to pass the Fitzgerald's divorce act before it was all over. Lida received $20,000 (a little over half a million today) a year in alimony, as well as a $300,000 ($7.6 million) trust fund for the couple's three young sons.

Lida, who was said to be worth a $1 million ($25 million now) and also extremely beautiful, was introduced to the prince at a ball in Dinard, one of France's top summer resorts for the rich and connected at that time. Adding to his complicated life, he'd ended up in Dinard trying to escape the very determined

Josephine. Being pursued didn't stop his search for a wealthy wife. Lida, having just successfully gotten a ton of money in her much-publicized divorce (which she added to the piles of cash she already had) was there to recuperate from the rigors of getting rid of a spouse. While Victor was courting her in the posh public rooms of the high-class hotel where they were staying, he was also carrying on an affair with another show girl—no, not our Baby Jo.

The prince's reputation had preceded him, and news stories reported she was at first aloof to his charms. But he followed her after her return to Uniontown, and Lida, as women have done for eons, began making excuses for his behavior.

"What the poor Prince needs is someone to take care of him," the *St. Louis Dispatch* reported in an article appearing on Sunday, December 20, 1914. "He is so open-handed that everyone imposes on his. He is not really bad—just careless."

Lida wouldn't marry him right away, though, making him wait three years or so. Finally she deemed him ready, saying, "He was born a Prince—that is neither his fault nor mine—but I shall make him a man. I shall pay his debts, re-establish him in life and watch over him with the solicitude of mother for the rest of his days. Watch and see."

Miss Lida Niccolls Is Wedded to a Prince
Divorced Wife of Gerald Fitzgerald Married in Uniontown, PA
Philadelphia Inquirer, November 2, 1911

Despite the objection of her millionaire uncle, J. V. Thompson, Miss Lida Niccolls, the divorced wife of Gerald Fitzgerald, mine and cattle king, was married this afternoon in the parlor of her mother's beautiful home in Uniontown, to Prince Victor of Thurn and Taxis. Miss Niccolls divorced Fitzgerald in England about three years ago after a sensational fight in the English and Irish courts.

In London she met the Prince several months ago. Miss Niccolls is the favorite niece of Mr. Thompson, the Uniontown coal and coke king who spent his money freely in aiding his niece to divorce the Irishman.

The Prince and his fiancée came to America, arriving in Pittsburgh last Saturday to get Mr. Thompson's consent to the wedding. The Prince registered at the Hotel Schenley, where he lived in the disguise of a tourist. Today he quietly went to Uniontown.

The wedding took place without Mr. Thompson's consent, nor was the uncle of the bride present. In fact, he did not know they had been married until this evening, when he was informed by a newspaper.

Lida's wealthy coal baron uncle, obviously a shrewd judge of character, didn't want his niece to marry a wastrel, whether he was a prince or not. He needn't have worried. Like our Minnie, though of course not of the same class or murderous disposition, Lida was no fool when it came to men. Besides the large chunk of her first husband's estate, as if that wasn't enough, she'd successfully battled and won—in a decade-long legal battle—her right to $35,000 annual income from Fitzgerald's US mine holdings. She wasn't about to be snookered by the prince. She most likely wanted his title and entrance to the most elite of aristocratic social circles. Who knows, she probably did think she could change him—don't women always think that? The wedding of the prince and the Uniontown heiress took place after a deed of separation had been drawn that ensured the new princess retained control of her American wealth.

Smart thinking, Lida.

As for Josephine, let's just say she wasn't happy about the situation at all now that the prince had taken another wife. But she wasn't about to give up and continued to call herself princess of Thurns and Taxis, which, as far as Lida was concerned, added up to one too many princesses.

Besides the wayward prince and the conniving Josephine, Lida had other difficulties as well. The year following her marriage, thieves stole $80,000 ($1.9 million) worth of jewelry from the hotel where she was staying in Ostend, Belgium. For some reason, it was decided by authorities that the famous American boxer Kid McCoy (i.e., in real life the less dramatically named

Norman Selby), who also had been staying at the hotel, was the thief. McCoy was arrested and jailed without bail. Though he denied knowing anything about the robbery, he remained locked up for a while before finally being allowed to return to New York. Once there, he filed suit against the government of Belgium for wrongful arrest, asking for $250,000.

"At the time I went to Ostend to spend the weekend, I didn't know there was any such person in the world as the Princess of Thurn and Taxis," he told reporters.

McCoy probably wished, after all that happened, he still didn't.

While $80,000 might seem like a lot of money in jewelry for most of us, Lida had been lucky. She had in her room assorted gems worth between $1 and $1.5 million, including a necklace reportedly valued at $400,000, or $10 million in today's money. Fortunately, the burglars were only able to swipe the few pieces she'd left scattered around on her dressing table. One might ask why anyone would leave such expensive jewelry carelessly laying around, but that's because they aren't a princess.

Next, Lida determined to put a stop to Josephine calling herself the princess of Thurn and Taxis. And as history will show, Lida was not one to mess with.

Wins Right to Use Title
Lida Eleanor Fitzgerald Is Princess, London Court Rules
Indianapolis News, Wednesday, December 2, 1914

The long-standing dispute of two American women, Lida Eleanor Fitzgerald and Josephine Moffitt, as to which was entitled to style herself Princess Victor Thurn and Taxis, was settled in the chancery court today in favor of Mrs. Fitzgerald. The court allowed Mrs. Fitzgerald $500 damages, gave her the cost of the trial and granted her an injunction against Miss Moffitt. The Prince in now serving in the Austrian Army.

Josephine didn't go down without a fight, arguing that non-royal Lida couldn't be a princess, as her marriage with Victor was morganic—one between people of unequal social rank, which prevents the passage of the husband's titles and privileges to the wife and any children born of the marriage.

There's a rare photo, on display at the Fayette County Public Library, showing Lida, princess of Thurn and Taxis; her son John Purcell Fitzgerald to the left; and her second husband, Prince Victor Theodore Maximillian Egon Maria Lamoral of Thurn and Taxis, on the right after their arrival in New York aboard the SS *Aquitania* from Europe in October 1927. It may seem like a happy family photo, but Prince Victor would die in Vienna early the next year at age fifty-two, and Lida and John would fight about his marriage to a model. Lida, in true domineering form, would sue to have the marriage annulled. That was one of many legal battles in her very glamorous but litigious life. Indeed, she outmatched both Lida and Minnie when it came to hiring lawyers. But people also sued her, including a fake count who, before he was unmasked, hung with the same crowd as Lida and her prince.

"Count" Asks $50,000 of Princess Victor
Gregory Charges Member of the Thurn
and Taxis Family Slandered Him
New York Times, May 9, 1920

Lida won this one and Gregory, a conman claiming to be an aristocrat, didn't get his $50,000 though Gregory went on to write some wonderfully catty articles about Lida and the Prince as well as other aristocratic types he'd met while masquerading as a count.

Lida spent the next decade or so mingling with the aristocratic set in the upper echelons of European society before she returned to the States to sue her son.

Princess Lida Loses Suit
Special Master Declares Son's Marriage Is Valid
New York Times, February 5, 1949

Former Princess Lida of Thurn and Taxis today lost her fight before a special master to have her 49-year-old son's marriage to a New York model annulled.

In his report, E. D. Brown, special master appointed by Fayette County Court, recommended that the petition be dismissed. The court will issue a decree later.

Mr. Brown said the marriage between John Purcell Fitzgerald and Eileen Simmons, aged 37, at Elkton, Md., late June 21 "is assented by them (the married couple) and is therefore a legal and lawful marriage under the laws of Maryland." He said, "The court is without authority to annul the marriage."

Princess Lida's petition said her son, heir to a Uniontown coal mining fortune, had been a habitual drunkard for ten years at the time of the ceremony and unable to comprehend the responsibilities of marriage.

We really shouldn't call her princess because Lida had given up her title the year before and resumed her American citizenship so she could fight her son in court. He, though, retained the title Sir John, earned from his father's family with its ancient Irish lineage. Though they never ranked as high as a prince, the Fitzgeralds did have more money and class than Lida's second husband and could count assorted viscountcies and baronetcies among their relatives.

Though Sir John got to keep Eileen Simpson Fitzgerald, his redheaded model, in 1949 she died suddenly at age thirty-seven in New York City, where the couple lived. Sir John was encouraged to sign the papers to have an autopsy performed to determine if she'd died of a heart condition. Eileen's body, Lida announced, would most likely be returned to her mother, Mabel Clark, in San Francisco.

Lida had a penchant for lawsuits, and she would spend the rest of her long life involved in many. But she was savvy and retained her fortune, spending her time between residences in New York, Uniontown, and various hotspots in Europe. After her death on December 6, 1965, at age ninety, her estate totaled $1,288,123 (after taxes it was a mere $659,333, or $6 million today) and went to her two surviving sons. The sheer number of her valuables was such that many had long been in storage in both Uniontown and at her home in London, which had been shuttered since 1914.

As for whether Lida made a man out of the prince or her uncle was right, we'll let you decide.

Princess Loses Husband's Estate
(*Connellsville, PA*) *Daily Courier*, Tuesday, April 1, 1930

Princess Lida Thurn-et-Taxis, who before her marriage at Uniontown, Pa., in 1911, was Lida Eleanor Fitzgerald, nee Nichols, of Pittsburg and Uniontown, lost her suit today to inherit all of the $2100 estate which her late husband, Prince Victor of Thurn-et-Taxis, willed to a Polish dancer.

Lida didn't really need the money—and she probably didn't like the prince much by then—but it must have annoyed her no end that Victor's Polish dancer would get even a very paltry $2,100.

As for Josephine, not much is heard of her after 1915, and what is wasn't good. There was a raid on her London apartment after neighbors reported loud music, gambling, and drinking. As this was typical of Josephine's style of entertaining, more police reports were to come.

The *London Times* reported on Saturday, January 29, 1915, that Josephine accused a man named Maur of attempting to blackmail her and acknowledged that he had frequently visited her in her apartment. Her representative referred to Josephine as princess of Thurn and Taxes, the wife of Prince Victor of Thurn and Taxis, her husband for some years. It didn't take long for Josephine's true identity to come out, and charges against Maur were dropped.

A few years later, a short article reported that Josephine was selling off her possessions.

Then she seems to disappear from the news. It's doubtful she had lived out her life in litigious splendor like Lida. Most likely she was like the majority of the other women chronicled in the *Inter Ocean* article in 1902—a swift rise and, though she hung on longer than most, a rapid fall. By the time we lose sight of her, she was in her mid-forties and trying to pass, often successfully, for twenty. Ultimately, she faded into obscurity and most likely poverty. But we always liked Josephine's spunk, and she never had to murder anyone to get what she wanted.

Unlike Baby Jo's, Minnie's saga wasn't close to done. Another wealthy man would die after ingesting poison, and there were more angry heirs and lawsuits to come.

9

OF PLUM JAM, CHAMPAGNE, WILLS, UNPAID BILLS, AND THE FINAL DEATH THAT WE KNOW OF

"MY GOD," MINNIE CALLED OUT TO HER GUESTS AFTER Dethlef Hansen barged into her home, stumbled past her, and then half fell into the dimly lit wine cellar. Glancing down, she saw the drunken lawyer with red splotches across his throat and brow. "More trouble for me, Hansen has killed himself."

Fortunately for Minnie, Hansen wasn't injured. Standing up, he wiped his forehead, and mumbled "plum jam is awful good; dish got broke."

Dethlef Hansen helped Minnie fake her marriage, obtain John Ketcham's signature on the will, bribe witnesses, and then negotiated with the family to settle the case, netting Minnie another $250,000 for a month or so of marriage—which seems to have been her going rate for marrying an old man. He may even have aided in hurrying Ketcham's death.

For a while, he'd lived with her; maybe they were lovers. But then she grew tired of him, not only kicking him out of her home and her life, but also stiffing him on legal fees, which dated back four years. Outraged, Hansen filed suit, saying she owed him $20,000 in legal fees.

It was back to court for Minnie. But it should come as no surprise that she once again had a wealthy champion—another rich, elderly man who was, of course, totally besotted by her.

Before Chicago Jury
Interesting Stories about the Well-Known Woman.
Lawyer Is Charged with Betraying His Client
Topeka State Journal, June 15, 1901

Mrs. Minnie Wallace Walkup Ketcham Is Now Having Trouble with Her Chicago Attorney Who Is Trying to Collect a Fee of $20,000.

A.S. Trude, attorney for Mrs. Ketcham, in the suit brought against her by Dethlef C. Hansen to collect $20,000 in attorney's fees, fanned himself with his handkerchief and made his opening statements to the jury in Judge Tuthill's court yesterday.

Hansen hounded Mrs. Ketcham, and Trude thundered in front of the judge, betrayed her as a client, and for a month and a half insisted on living in her house, drinking her dead husband's champagne and eating her plum jam. And now he was asking for $20,000 in alleged lawyer's fees. Trude's strategy was to belittle Hansen's abilities as a lawyer as well as make Hansen look like an incompetent clown.

It turned out to be a fairly heated courtroom battle.

Attorney F. E. Gray testified about first meeting Minnie when Hansen invited him to dinner at her home. Minnie told Gray that Hansen was such a hard worker, slaving away on her case day and night, that he was staying at her house. As Hansen, despite his failings, was young and handsome, there might have been other reasons why he was part of Minnie's household, but that wasn't brought up during the discussion.

"You didn't see any of Hansen's legal services, did you?" he was asked by Minnie's attorney.

"Nothing but the dinner service," replied Gray.

"Well did you see anything of the plum jelly which later came to a mysterious end at Hansen's hands?" was the next question.

Hansen's attorney, Hugo Pam, objected.

"All right," Trude replied. "I withdraw the jelly. Mr. Clerk, strikeout the jam."

Pam, still upset, began pacing back and forth and shook a warning finger at Mr. Trude.

"You know the tricks, you old bird," he said.

"I object to his calling me a bird, your honor" was Trude's reply.

For his part, Hansen described his former client as one of the shrewdest women in the world, noting that she had a way of crying in court that could soften the hardest heart.

"I was Mrs. Ketcham's attorney three years ago, after she had been acquitted of the murder of her first husband and had married John B. Ketcham. Mr. and Mrs. Ketcham lived at 3421 Indiana Avenue. He was a well-known Chicago clubman. It was expected by some that she would be tried on a charge of murdering her second husband also, but I conducted the case and no charge was ever brought."

Hansen recalled that he and Minnie first met early in 1897, when she, using the last name of Wallace, came to his office, asking for help in evading payment of a $600 dressmaking bill she owed to a New Orleans store. Later she'd turn to him for help in all things Ketcham. Hansen was a staunch ally and spoke up for her, in attempts to manipulate public opinion. But in the courtroom he told the real story.

Wedding and the Will
Chicago Tribune, Friday, June 14, 1901

"Minnie Wallace came into my office one day in August 1897," said Hansen. "She wanted to know how she could get his [Ketcham's] bonds out of his safety deposit box. I told her to get an order from him and the password to the safe. Another time she wanted to know how much Ketcham was worth, and remarked she didn't know how long 'the old fool' would live.

"About September 15 she said she didn't think Ketcham would live long. She feared a Chicago wedding might start the newspapers to raking up her Kansas career. I advised her to take Ketcham to Milwaukee, register under assumed names, and get married. On October 1 she came to my office and said she had married Ketcham. At this time, she spoke of a will, but expressed doubts whether she could induce the old man to sign one.

Together the two succeeded at getting Ketcham's signature on a will that left his entire estate to her. Helping them was Minnie's longtime maid, Mrs. Torrey, who also was her mother's cousin, and the ever-faithful Keller, both of whom acted as witnesses.

On November 15, Hansen returned to his office to find a note under his door telling him of Ketcham's death and summoning him to the house. Arriving he found the place filled with reporters and the police.

Minnie hired Hansen to defend her against what would happen once her real name and past were discovered. As they talked, Gladys Forbes arrived in a cab. Rushing up to Minnie, Forbes threw her arms around her, stating that she'd already talked to an attorney and he'd see nothing happened to her. Upset, Hansen pulled Minnie aside and warned if the reporters inside her home saw the notorious Gladys, "it would be all over."

Besides a visit by Gladys, there was more dirt to be dug up. Several newspapers ran stories about how Minnie, under an assumed name, rented a separate residence where she entertained men and served liquor (which they knew because she skipped out on paying the bill). When Hansen confronted her about it, Minnie told him the story was true.

This is what Hansen had to deal with in saving Minnie from another murder trial: contend with her unsavory acquaintances, such as Gladys Forbes; downplay she'd been tried for the murder of her first husband; and make sure the Ketcham family didn't prove that John hadn't been the bridegroom in Milwaukee and that the will had been forged. Oh, and somehow make people overlook that while Ketcham was dying, Minnie had men visiting her in rented rooms down the street. It was a daunting assignment. But in the end, no charges were filed, and Minnie got her money.

Attorney Trude Claims Forgery
Claims Eliged Note from Mrs. Ketcham Show In Court is Forged
Laughter Still Rings
Plantiff Testifies and Is Called a Betrayer of Professional Secrets
Becomes Excited on Stand
Chicago Tribune, Friday, June 14, 1901

"My dear: Will you kindly write me about the law in regard to debt—how long it takes to outlaw debts in Illinois and in Louisiana. With love and good wishes. AS EVER."

As Hansen was reading a letter aloud in the courtroom, purported to have been written by Minnie about trying to evade some of the numerous debts she had occurred, she grew visibly angry, her cheeks reddened, and her eyes flashed. She pointed a white-gloved finger at Hansen while telling Trude that her former lawyer was lying. Trude loudly declared the letter a forgery though it was in her handwriting and on her stationery.

But Hansen at that point wasn't deterred by her hostility and told the court that he'd kept her from facing another murder charge by getting the Milwaukee minister to change his story about the groom looking like Joe Keller.

Poor Hansen. He was devious, but she was even more so, and, remember, she was the Winter Queen. He crumbled.

Lawyer Hansen Weeps in Court
Breaks Down in Trial of Suit for $20,000 Against Mrs. Ketcham.
On the Stand All Day.
Many Sensational Incidents During
Direct and Cross Examinations.
Chicago Daily Tribune, Saturday, June 15, 1901

Worn out by the mental and physical strain that he had been undergoing in the trial of his suit for fees, Dethlef C. Hansen broke down while on the witness stand yesterday morning and sobbed bitterly as in a broken voice he tried to tell why he had not invited the present defendant, Mrs. Minnie Wallace Ketcham and ex-Judge Shope to lunch in a downtown restaurant. He looked wan and weak when he entered the courtroom. His eyes were bloodshot and he clinched his hands nervously as he underwent the searching examination of the lawyers. About noon the break came.

Mr. Hansen had been telling of his attempt to get Mr. Shope to defend Mrs. Ketcham on the charge of being implicated in the death of John B. Ketcham.

"Why did you not have Judge Shope dine with you and Mrs. Ketcham downtown when you wanted him to enter the case, instead of taking his to the Ketcham house?" asked Attorney Pam.

"Because," he sobbed, "I did not want to parade her in a public hotel. Crowds followed her everywhere and I wanted to save her the notoriety."

A touch of her old liking for the attorney must have come back, or perhaps a feeling of pity, but whatever it was Mrs. Ketcham's face softened and she looked on Hansen with kindlier interest than at any time during the trial. So did Judge Tuthill and the attorneys for they gave him several minutes to recover his composure.

It was just a short break from the high-pitched courtroom battle. Before long, Trude was accusing Hansen of stealing Minnie's letters. Hansen rose from the witness stand, screaming, "I did not, I did not!"

Trude responded just as vehemently, swearing to defend Minnie and adding, "I will make your fur and feathers fly before I am done with you."

Attorney Harry Hurd, who was assisting Pam, objected. Judge Tuthill said the objection was noted.

"I don't want it noted," exclaimed Hurd. "I want a ruling."

But he didn't get one, and court was adjourned until the following Tuesday.

Unbelievably, it got weirder as the trial went on. Miss Jennie C. Naracon, a stenographer at the Mooney & Boland Detective Agency, testified she'd hidden under the bed at the Indiana Avenue house to eavesdrop. Unfortunately, because of her cramped position, she couldn't take notes.

Like Minnie's trial in Emporia, people stood in line to get a seat. It, like many things in her life, was quite a show.

The two eventually settled out of court. Hansen didn't get $20,000 but did end up with $3,000, though Minnie protested against paying. Whether she ever did isn't known.

Hansen would continue to work as a lawyer and to sue his clients. In March 1910, he filed a suit in the Supreme Court of the District of Columbus against multimillionaire Thomas W. Walsh, who discovered one of the largest gold mines in America, for one-quarter of a million dollars, alleging libel and conspiracy. The suit had its origins when the very young Violette Watson, supposedly a Parisian schoolgirl who was "adopted" by Walsh when he was commissioner for the United States during the Paris Exposition. It was one of those complicated breach-of-promise actions like Josephine's with Billie Pike (and later Prince Victor). Dethlef represented Violette, who'd grown up to become a showgirl. Violette claimed Walsh had promised to marry her, though he was already married to someone else and was in his fifties (she was sixteen when their romance began), pledging to pay $15,000 a year until the marriage happened. Loaded with cash and costly jewelry, Violette moved to New York. Walsh was already in the United States renting the Vanderbilt Newport Mansion, Beaulieu (not to be confused with the Breakers, another Vanderbilt mansion in Newport) for $100,000.

Walsh, we can assume, never planned on leaving his wife, and Watson soon realized that and decided to sue. She contacted Hansen, promising him 40 percent of whatever he could collect. Their expectations were high—adding up to almost $1 million. Violette, though, double-crossed her attorney and negotiated her own settlement with Walsh for $55,000. Like Minnie, she then refused to pay Hansen the 40 percent. Hansen's complicated attempt to get his money led to his almost being disbarred, and he wasn't allowed to practice for a year. We don't know what happened to Violette, but Walsh continued living the lush life (and, one might assume, continued "adopting other young school girls"). Evalyn, his only surviving daughter, made a brilliant marriage. Her husband, Edward Beale "Ned" McLean, owner and publisher of the *Washington Post*, was also a Thoroughbred racehorse owner who bought the Hope diamond. Unfortunately for him, the Hope diamond curse prevailed, and he died in a psychiatric hospital.

As for Minnie, she already had her hooks in another rich old geezer who should have known better.

The two met when robber baron extraordinaire DeLancy Louderback and his wife of over three decades, Virginia, were attending a ball held in one of Chicago's fashionable hotels. The first sight of Minnie, dressed in a brightly colored peacock gown, her black hair bound in a band of emeralds, inflamed him and infuriated his wife.

"But she is divine—divine," he told a friend while Mrs. Louderback, a noted figure in Chicago society, left the ball in tears.

Hook, line, and sinker, Minnie had landed a big catch in Louderback.

Before long, Minnie had sold her Indiana Avenue home and was living at the Grand Pacific Hotel, where she and the millionaire were seen together frequently—without Mrs. Louderback.

While Minnie was battling Dethlef Hansen, her former attorney, in court, she was also often accompanied by Louderback and at times went to stay in his palatial New York home protected by detectives he'd hired. People talked, but what did Minnie care? There was nothing that could be said about her behavior that hadn't been said before.

As for Louderback, he was off-the-wall afraid she'd leave him for someone else. "Every man in the world was conspiring to take her," he told people, and so to protect his love from the temptation of a younger, or at least richer, man, he built her a house. This wasn't your usual type of mansion, according to a *Washington Times* story that described it:

> The construction of this extraordinary monument to a man's insane infatuation and insane jealousy must have cost him nearly a million dollars. It is literally a house within a house. The outer shell was built of massive stone, whose strength and thickness was not apparent on looking at the exterior. Windows and doors are reinforced with steel. And within this is the inside house.

This house is separated from the outer shell by a space large enough to enable a man to walk everywhere between and also to allow guards to be in place there if necessary. Within this space are said to have been built secret passages, loopholes, listening posts and all the mechanism for surveillance and espionage that a jealous Sultan with an ingenious mind might have devised to keep watch upon his favorite Sultana.

The interior home was over seven thousand square feet, and it was three stories tall. The entire structure, outer shell and interior, took up one city block.

While the home was being built, DeLancy and Minnie did some serious shopping for an estimated $1 million in furnishings, earning what had been called the "House of Mystery" a new name: "Paradise Palace." What happened next isn't exactly known, except that Minnie decided she didn't want to move into this double-walled house. Instead, she left Chicago, moving into a lavish home on East Eighty-Eighth Street in New York that Louderback had also furnished for her. Later she would move to England.

If Louderback hoped to marry her when his wife died, which she finally got around to doing, he was to be disappointed. Shortly before he was to leave to join her in London, Louderback received a cable from Minnie stating she had married a Captain Keating. Little is known about this third husband or if he even existed, but Minnie would wax poetic about this great love of hers later when the *Washington Times* did a rehash of her romantic career.

Louderback was indeed moving to London, but was he really planning on marrying Minnie, who was almost fifty? Would he have committed suicide if she had married someone else? And he hadn't quite rushed into marriage, as his wife had died two years previously. There were other—much younger—women.

Agnes Sowka, et al.

As taken as he was with Minnie, Louderback still had an eye for the ladies. Agnes Sowka was a twenty- (or twenty-one-, depending on the news account) year-old stenographer involved with her boss, a married con man named Harvey Hill, when the sixty-one-year-old Louderback invited her to dinner. She agreed, she said later, because she thought he was a lonely old man. The two knew each other because she worked in an office near his. After dinner, Louderback suggested they go to an apartment he kept on the north side, and so she did. What happened next was a boon to the attorneys hired by each side to sort it out.

Louderback Sued for $25,000
Twenty-Year-Old Stenographer Accuses Him of Breach of Promise
(Chicago) Inter Ocean, Sunday, October 27, 1913

DeLancy Louderback, a millionaire real estate dealer, was made defendant in a suit filed yesterday for $25,000 by Miss Agnes Sowka, a 20-year-old stenographer living at 4511 North Forty Fourth Court.

Mr. Louderback last night refused to discuss the charge. His attorney, Fletcher Dobyns, would only say: "It's a simple case of blackmail; that's all."

We're not sure what the breach of promise charge was all about, but maybe DeLancy promised Agnes something more than sweet nothings for spending time alone in the apartment with him.

A settlement was said to have been reached, but then the file disappeared—most likely stolen by friends of Louderback or Sowka—so there was no record of the agreement. Of course, it could have accidentally been misplaced, but we tend to doubt that. This was Chicago after all. We hope Agnes got her money.

Turned out Agnes had a bit of a past herself. On May 6, 1913, the *Chicago Tribune* reported that Agnes and Hill along with Louderback had traveled frequently together, staying in hotels together (we're not going there). The three were at the luxurious newly opened West Baden resort in Indiana while Mrs. Hill was in the hospital delivering a baby. One of the more scandalous anecdotes about Agnes, as reported by the *Tribune*, was when Hill asked for money to pay the chauffeur: "Miss Sowka, in the presence of an interested crowd, removed the fare from her stocking."

Despite these other women, Louderback kept Minnie in his will.

Noted Beauty Left Fortune by Louderback
Mrs. Minnie Ketcham Whose Two Husbands
Died by Poison Gets Fourth of Estate
Jilts Capitalist by Cable
Refusal Comes Few Days before Death of
Associate of Yerkes from Toxic Cause
Chicago Examiner, April 19, 1914

For more than ten years there was a hidden romance in the life of DeLancy Louderback but the identity of the woman on whom he was lavishing money remained a secret until yesterday with the filing of the Louderback will in the probate court. The closely cherished secret of the man who made millions was published to the world. Mrs. Minnie Wallace Walkup Ketcham is to receive one-fourth of the entire estate for her use during her lifetime.

The only other bequest in the will of similar magnitude is the one-fourth left for Sarah E. Ritter, a half-sister who has managed the Louderback home since the death of Mrs. Louderback two years ago. Clarissa Boehnkin of St. Louis gets one-fourth less certain bequests including $3,000 for Miss Bertha A. Schneider, Mr. Louderback's private secretary, and Hilda M. Brand, his nurse who receives $500. Three nieces, Marjorie and Susan Braun and Marie Hopkinson of Philadelphia, get equal shares in the last fourth. The estate provides against contest. Attached to the will, as if he foresaw dissatisfaction among the beneficiaries, DeLancy Louderback put the following stipulation: "if any person or persons named herein shall claim out of my estate any other or greater interest or portion than I herein give such person or persons who shall in any way contest this my last will and testament then such person or persons shall be given $1 and no more."

The Minnie Wallace Walkup Ketcham named in the Louderback will has had a bizarre past worthy of attention for the student of psychology and coincidence. Twice she has been married. Each time her husband has died in mysterious circumstances. Once she has been tried for murder of the first husband and now DeLancy Louderback, millionaire builder of the union loop, fellow-worker of Yerkes in the monumental rehabilitation of Chicago's traction system, is dead of poison.

The will further stipulated that after Clariss Boehnkin's death, the money left to her was to be divided between her two daughters, Olga and Susie. Sarah Ritter got a life interest, but it's not known who received her share after her death. Describing Minnie in his will as "my friend," Louderback left her share for life only, and after her death one-half would go to his niece, Jean D. Louderback of Oakland, California, and the remaining half to other heirs. We hope that Jean D. Louderback was very young because Minnie would live for another forty some years.

Defends Silence on Death

M. J. Faherty Takes Blame in Louderback Case
Dr. Kelly Still Won't Talk
Refuses to Say Whether Stomach Was Washed Out

M. J. Faherty, a Ravenswood real estate man, admittedly closer to the late DeLancy H. Louderback, capitalist, than members of the dead man's family, yesterday asserted if there had been a mistake in suppressing the facts as to Mr. Louderback's death, he was to blame.

Faherty made the statement in defense of his protégé and neighbor, Dr. Paul Kelly, who was with Mr. Louderback when death came.

Dr. Kelly would not say if he had washed the stomach of the dead or dying man to hide traces of a possible mistake.

Used Sleeping Pills Extensively

"Six years ago a druggist to me Mr. Louderback used five times the amount of insomnia potion that any man he ever heard of took," Faherty said.

"Louderback is dead now, being buried today; let him alone," Faherty continued. "He has no widow or children. Dr. Kelly has nothing to tell."

"Why doesn't he say if he used a stomach pump, what he diagnosed Mr. Louderback's trouble to be, and what medicines, if any, he used?"

Gives Theory of Death

"Paul is a fine boy. If he doesn't want to answer he doesn't have to. I am reasonably certain Mr. Louderback took an overdose of this sleeping dope he was in the habit of using. That can be the worst you newspapers can dig up."

Not that it much mattered. Call it the incredible shrinking fortune. Just like Ketcham, Louderback had lost most of his fortune. Part of it went to Minnie, including at least $3 million in cash, as well as expensive clothes, jewels, carriages and horses, trips, expensive stays in grand hotels, and whatever else such a beauty deserved, including a magnificent mansion on East Eighty-Eighth Street in New York, which he also lavishly furnished for her. Added to that was the "house within a house" in Ravenswood, which cost more than $1 million, not including another million or so in furnishings. That all begins to add up.

At the time of his "accidental" death, early news reports indicated Louderback's fortune had gone from $4 million just a few years previously to $100,000. But in 1914 dollars, that still was a lot of money—a little over $2.4 million now. But for the heirs, the news got worse.

Louderback's Estate Less Than $10,000
Mrs. Minnie Ketcham's Share Will Be Under
$1, Ending Likelihood of Contest
Chicago Examiner, April 29, 1914

The filing of an inventory yesterday of the estate of DeLancy H. Louderback, reputed millionaire and former associate of Charles T. Yerkes, revealed that the vast wealth of the retired capitalist had shrunk to less than $10,000 at the time of his death three weeks ago. The beneficiaries under the provisions of the will with possibility two exceptions will receive only cents. The two who probably will receive their full shares are Miss. Bertha A. Schneider, Louderback's private secretary who is given $5000 and Hilda M. Brand, his nurse who is bequeathed $500. Mrs. Minnie Wallace Walkup Ketcham, the presence of whose name in the will revealed a hidden romance in the life of Louderback, is to get one-fourth of the residue of the estate after the special bequests have been satisfied. She is among the beneficiaries whose share will hardly reach one dollar according to attorney John H. Cummings Jr., for years Louderback's counsel and sole executor under the terms of the will. The estate as filed yesterday consists of these items: $4000 in the bank, $300 in Traveler's Express company checks, $100 life insurance policy, $1400 of a small real estate trust fund. Mr. Cummings declared that there was no real estate in Louderback's name.

Lost Money in Panic Year

As things look now, the estate will run considerably under $10,000 after all the personal debts of Mr. Louderback are paid, said Mr. Cummings. Mr. Louderback was a very wealthy man some 15 years ago about the time the Northwestern Elevated was completed in 1907. However he suffered heavy losses in industrial stocks.

Coincidental with the move to settle the Louderback estate it became known yesterday that Miss Agnes Sowka at 7:00 o'clock this evening will wed Joseph A. Nitz, a salesman. In October of 1912, Miss Sowka filed suit for $25,000 damages against Mr. Louderback. Miss Sowka, then 21 years old, made serious charges against Louderback. The action was settled out of court.

Minnie wasn't done with lawsuits. In March 1915, she sued the Louderback estate for $2550 because of four checks the late magnate had written to her before he died that had never been cashed. The article also noted that Minnie planned to return to Chicago and take up residence in the "house within a house." But that wasn't to be.

The House within the House Redux

After his death, Louderback's home sat empty for almost two years until an old friend purchased it. Unfortunately it has since been torn down.

Louderback Mansion Is Again Aglow
17 Months of Darkness and a Famous House Within a House;
Neighbors Stirred
Michael J. Faherty Purchases Memento of Old
Friend as an Investment and Entertains.
Chicago Examiner, Wednesday September 8, 1915

17 months of silence have covered the house within the house at 4918 North Bernard Ave., where DeLancy Louderback, who made

millions in traction deals and spent most of it before he died, used to live in lonesome state.

But last night lights blazed forth from every window. Music floated out. Automobiles chugged and buzzed up to the drive. Men and women, some in high hats and upper cloaks, others in derbies and caps and start and "middle blouse" outfit, thronged the house in the grounds.

Crowds Gather

The neighbors for blocks around flock to the iron fence that surrounded the great grounds of the old Louderback mansion.

"Somebody's bought the place for a new casino," suggested one.

"No," said another, "it's to be a gambling den. Don't you see the cards and the tables on the porch?"

"You're all wrong so the third, it's to be a new country club or roadhouse, 'cause I saw a keg of beer hauled in there this afternoon."

But nobody guessed it. Here's the explanation. He [Faherty] had bought the house and grounds and was entertaining some 200 of his million friends at a "housewarming."

A case of sentiment

"I bought the place because of its association," said Saturday. "I spent many happy carefree evenings here with DeLancy Louderback when he was alive and I did not want to see the house within the house that going to other hands, perhaps to be dismantled. I shall keep it, let us say, as an investment, but I don't think I will move away from my own home to the twenty-third ward."

"Maybe Roger, your son, is going to be married and live in the house?" suggested one.

"It isn't impossible," admitted the host, "but I don't talk about that."

Inside, judges Aldermen and others danced and sang to the music of the Victrola or the orchestra. Upstairs in the room that had been DeLancy Louderback's bedroom, an impromptu bar was set up and a white apron dispenser was in charge.

The wide glassed-in porches where Louderback used to spend much of his time were set with card tables.

Noted as landmark

The "house within a house" had long been one of the sights of the Ravenswood subdivision. When Louderback built it the house proper was first constructed, and then the entire lower floors were incased in the glass porches that ran around the front sides. The grounds cover a city block. The estimated value of the property is $1 million. When the mansion was completed it was claimed that Louderback contemplated marriage and that Minnie Wallace Ketcham, famous in three other marriages and millionaires, was to become the mistress of the place.

After his death, it was found that the estate had been divided but that one-fourth had been willed to Mrs. Ketcham.

How Louderback died was of utmost importance to his heirs.

The coroner's office convened a grand jury and an autopsy was performed, though unfortunately Louderback's doctor had ordered his stomach pumped when he grew so ill, and then after his death, he'd been embalmed. Still, death was attributed to an overdose of cyanimide, a cyanide compound that has been used as a fertilizer and defoliant and, in many manufacturing processes, taken medicinally.

Besides Minnie's cable, another argument for suicide was based on the rumor that DeLancy had purchased extensive holdings along the line of the proposed subway and had then become depressed when that project was defeated at the election Tuesday. Others denied this.

Many believed that Minnie had somehow set it up so he would take the poison, thinking it was a sleeping draft or that coconspirators had helped engineer the fatal dose.

That's one of the theories put forth by Virginia A. McConnell, who chronicled Minnie's life in *The Adventuress* and believes the likely suspects were Minnie, Sally Ritter, and her son, Henry Jr.—the latter two since they took care of his house as well as him giving them easy access to his medications.

One newspaper reported that Minnie supplied Louderback with the many sleeping powders he took to combat insomnia. Cyanimide was also used to cure alcoholism. Could Minnie have encouraged him to take it because of that? Well, we think so.

Dobyns, his attorney since the Sowka suit, was quoted in the *Roth Island Argus* and *Daily Union* on Saturday, April 11, 1914, as saying, "From what I know of his personal affairs, they were in good shape. He was not of the suicidal disposition, and he would have been the one man I should've picked out to be free of such inclination."

DeLancy had been making plans to move to London, where Minnie was living. If Dobyns was correct about his finances, then there was a great deal of money and/or property missing.

Could Minnie have somehow finagled him into giving it to her to hold on to? Would you have put it past her? Some thought so. But then, so many people were so cynical about Minnie's motives.

McConnell also points out that each time one of Minnie's men died, there was a young man in the house: Willie Willis when Walkup died of arsenical poisoning; Joe Keller (and to some extent Dethlef Hansen) when Ketcham perished from too much drink or, maybe, a pillow pushed over his face as he slept; and finally Harry Ritter when Louderback swallowed his draught.

And consider this: each time a wealthy old codger dropped dead and left Minnie money, her technique improved. She faced the gallows after the death of James Walkup. When Ketcham died, there was an inquest, a battle with his family for her inheritance, rumors of fraud, impersonation, and imprisoning him, but not one accused her of murder. This time, Minnie was an ocean away when Louderback "accidently" swallowed poison. Could it be a coincidence? Sure. Do we think so? Not a chance.

We think Minnie had perfected her game.

Epilogue: A Mystery to the Very End

Lives and fortune were squandered so Minnie could live a luxurious life. Whether she was able to keep up the high living after Louderbach's death, we don't know. As much as she loved charming reporters, she let herself disappear mostly from sight.

We catch a glimpse of her when she applied for a new passport on December 18, 1914, under the name Ketcham, and listed her permanent residence as London 20, Stratford Place. By 1930, she appeared to be living in Chicago in the Drexel Building.

There is, of course, another mystery: Estella Minnie Keating (Estella Minnie Lee), who was born on the same day as our Minnie, is listed in the US Social Security Applications and Claims Index, 1936–2007. But her father's name is listed as James Lee and her mother's as Elizabeth Middleton. Minnie's birthplace, which her birth certificate states is New Orleans, here says Richmond, Virginia—a location that has appeared in other documents regarding her.

It most likely is her—same name, same birthdate, same first names of parents. As usual it's mystery.

Ten years before she died, she moved to San Diego, where she died of heart failure at age eighty-eight on May 10, 1957. There is no marker on her grave, just as she never had one placed on either Dora or Elizabeth's graves. There's no indication of why she moved to California, having called Chicago, New Orleans, London, and New York her homes for so many years.

The name on her death certificate is strange—"Estelle (aka Estella) Minnie Keating (aka Ketchum)"—the latter being misspelled. Why she moved to San Diego we don't know. There were some members of Dora's family living in the area; her great-grandnephew remembered going to her funeral but didn't remember meeting her when she was alive. Besides, it's hard to envision even an aged Minnie spending time with little children.

As more and more records come online, maybe more of her past will be repealed, including whether Captain Keating really existed. We do know she said he'd died. Was that one more murder to add to her score?

BIBLIOGRAPHY

Abbott, Karen. *Sin in the Second City: Madams, Minister, Playboys, and the Battle for America's Soul.* New York: Random House, 2007.

Ancestry.com.

Curious Traveler's Guide to Route 66 in Metro Chicago. http://www .railsplitting.com.

The Esoteric Curiosa. http://theesotericcuriosa.blogspot.com.

Familysearch.com.

MacColl, Gail. *To Marry an English Lord: Tales of Wealth and Marriage, Sex and Snobbery.* New York: Workman Publishing Company, 2012.

McClelland, Edward. "The Most Corrupt Public Official in Illinois History: William Hale Thompson." NBC Chicago, January 25, 2012. http://www.nbcchicago.com/blogs/ward-room/The-Most -Corrupt-Public-Official-In-Illinois-History-William-Hale -Thompson-138057708.html#ixzz4nfkIt2wa.

McConnell, Virginia. *The Adventuress: Murder, Blackmail, and Confidence Games in the Gilded Era.* Kent, OH: Kent University, 2010.

Murder by Gaslight. http://www.murderbygaslight.com.

NOLA Crime Index: Times-Picayune. http://www.nola.com.

Sally Asher Arts. http://sallyasherarts.com.

Search of Our Past: Women of Northwest Ohio. Vol. 2. Toledo, OH: Women's History Committee of the Women Alive! Coalition, 1990.

St. Estephe. "Minnie Walkup Ketcham, Champion Gold-Digger Vamp Black Widow–1914." *The Unknown History of Misandry*, September 24, 2011. http://unknownmisandry.blogspot.com/2011/09 /minnie-walkup-ketcham-champion-gold.html.

United States census.

Wikipedia.

Newspapers

Asheville (NC) Citizen-Times
(Bird City, KS) Frontiersman
Brooklyn Daily Eagle
Chicago Daily Tribune
Chicago Examiner
(Chicago) Inter Ocean
Chicago Tribune
Cincinnati Enquirer
Decatur (IL) Daily Republican
Decatur (IL) Herald
Delaware County (PA) Daily Times
Emporia Daily News
Emporia Weekly News
Fort Scott (KS) Weekly
(Indianapolis, IN) Indianian
Indianapolis News
(Louisville, KY) Courier Journal
(Minneapolis) Star Tribune
New York Times
Salt Lake Herald-Republican
Sedalia Weekly Bazoo
(Shreveport, LA) Times
St. Joseph (MO) Gazette-Herald
St. Louis Post-Dispatch
Times-Picayune
Toledo State Journal
Topeka Daily Capitol
Vicksburg (MS) Evening Post
Washington Post
Wichita Daily Eagle
The (New York) World

Ever since she started her own newspaper at age eight, selling it to neighbors who had no choice but to subscribe, **Jane Simon Ammeson** has loved to write. She has now upped her game by writing about travel, food, murders, and history for newspapers, magazines, and websites and is author of thirteen books, including the recently released *Lincoln Road Trip*, *Hauntings of the Underground Railroad: Ghosts of the Midwest*, and *Murders That Made Headlines: Crimes of Indiana*. She also authored *A Jazz Age Murder in Northwest Indiana*, a true crime book about a murder that took place in her hometown. She authors a weekly food column for the *Herald Palladium* and Shelf Life, a book column for the *Times* of Northwest Indiana, and currently has three Bindu Travel Apps: Michigan Road Trips, Experience Curacao, and Indiana Journeys.

A James Beard Foundation judge (we told you she likes food) as well as a member of the Society of American Travel Writers (SATW) and Midwest Travel Journalists Association (MTJA), Jane makes her home base on the shores of Lake Michigan in southwest Michigan. Follow Jane on Facebook at janesimonammeson; Twitter @HPAmmeson and @travelfoodIN; and on her blogs, *Will Travel for Food* for the *Times* of Northwest Indiana (nwitimes.com/blogs /community), and janeammeson.blog.